R G MENZIES ESSAY

GAME PLAN

THE CASE FOR A NEW AUSTRALIAN GRAND STRATEGY

ROSS BABBAGE

MENZIES
RESEARCH
CENTRE

connorcourt
PUBLISHING

Connor Court Publishing Pty Ltd

Copyright © Ross Babbage 2015

ALL RIGHTS RESERVED. This book contains material protected under International and Federal Copyright Laws and Treaties. Any unauthorised reprint or use of this material is prohibited. No part of this book may be reproduced or transmitted in any form or by any means, electronic or mechanical, including photocopying, recording, or by any information storage and retrieval system without express written permission from the publisher.

PO Box 224W
Ballarat VIC 3350
sales@connorcourt.com
www.connorcourt.com

ISBN: 9781925138634 (pbk)

Cover design by Ian James

Printed in Australia

*To every good citizen the State owes
not only a chance in life but a self-respecting life.*

Robert Menzies[1]

---

1 R. G. Menzies, *The Forgotten People*, Angus and Robertson Ltd., Sydney, 1943, p. 47.

Contents

About the R. G. Menzies Essays of Ideas vi

About the author vii

Foreword – Nick Cater viii

Introduction 1

1. Grand Strategy and Its Evolution in Australia 5

2. Twelve Drivers of New Grand Strategy 13

3. Goals 49

4. Foundational Judgements 53

5. Options 63

6. Twelve Steps to Implementation 73

    Conclusions 89

    Acknowledgments 93

R. G. Menzies Essays of Ideas

Sir Robert Gordon Menzies kept a journal throughout his political life in which he would take notes of ideas, conversations and events.

The *R. G. Menzies Essays of Ideas* is published in the same spirit. It does not set out to be the last word on any given topic, merely a record of good ideas, articulately expressed, that may be enriched through further discussion.

If you would like to contribute to the debate online; or submit a contribution for future volumes, email: correspondence@menziesrc.org

Menzies Research Centre

Chairman: Tom Harley

Executive Director: Nick Cater

Deputy Director: Kay Gilchrist

PO Box 6091, Kingston, ACT 2604

Australia

Tel +61 2 6273 5608

Email: correspondence@menziesrc.org

www.menziesrc.org

About the Author

Ross Babbage is Managing Director of Strategy International (ACT) Pty Ltd. He is also Chair of the Academic Council of the Australian Business Academy, a member of Accenture's Advisory Board, a member of the Academic Advisory Council of the Menzies Research Centre and Founder of the Kokoda Foundation, the predecessor of the Institute for Regional Security.

Dr Babbage served for 16 years in the Australian Public Service holding several senior positions, including Head of Strategic Analysis in the Office of National Assessments and leading the branches in the Department of Defence responsible for ANZUS and global strategic policy and then Force Development. During the 1990s he held senior executive positions with ADI Ltd. In 2001 he was appointed to lead the Centre for International Strategic Analysis in Perth and in 2003 and 2004 he served as Head of the Strategic and Defence Studies Centre at the Australian National University. Dr Babbage was a special advisor to the Minister for Defence during the preparation of the 2009 Australian defence white paper. He also served on the Council of the International Institute for Strategic Studies in London for a maximum six year term. He was appointed a Member of the Order of Australia in 2011.

Foreword

The gravest challenge faced by this and any government is not balancing the Budget but defending the Australian people and their borders. Ross Babbage's contribution to the R. G. Menzies Essays series offers a sobering assessment of the multiple threats to national security for which we must prepare.

Never in the history of Australia has the challenge been more complex. We live in an era of strategic disruption in which the old certainties no longer apply. The rise of China and the belligerence of North Korea are powerful dynamics that dominate regional security. The toxic threat of radical Islamist ideology, the instability it is causing in the Middle East, the rise of non-state actors and the emergence of a dangerous domestic terrorist menace demand a thorough reassessment of our defence and wider national security capability.

The evolving outlook of our strategic allies, principally the United States and the strengthening of trade in Asia, are changing the international landscape. The rapid development of technology, its potential to be deployed against us, and the challenges of cyber-security also command attention.

Babbage presents a clear argument that the times demand a new Grand Strategy to serve as an overarching framework for national defence. This grand plan must take account of the new uncertainties while standing firmly by our tried and tested principles and alliances.

A new Grand Strategy must be capable of weighing the catastrophic yet unlikely threat of serious coercion or major attack on Australian soil against the more likely but less consequential possibility of internal instability in the Pacific. It must encompass Australia's global responsibility for the defence of freedom and incorporate the related challenge of national security.

The Coalition government's commitment to increase defence spending to two per cent of Gross Domestic Product within a decade is recognition of the scale of the challenge. It is vital, however, that Australia's investment in defence is based on sound principles. Goals must be agreed and priorities set if an enlarged but finite defence budget is to effectively increase our capability.

The Menzies Research Centre publishes Babbage's essay in the certain knowledge that not everyone will agree with its conclusions and in the hope that it will provoke robust discussion on these vital matters.

Nick Cater
Executive Director
Menzies Research Centre
June 2015

Introduction

Australia's strategic landscape is more challenging now than at any time since the Second World War. China is rising to become the largest global economy with formidable military capabilities. Of particular concern is that the regime in Beijing is pursuing assertive nationalist strategies abroad, largely in an effort to sustain its legitimacy.

A notable example is China's declaration of sovereignty over more than 80 per cent of the South China Sea, extending more than 900 nautical miles from the Chinese coast. In order to strengthen Beijing's hold on these disputed waters, the Chinese have been dredging vast quantities of sand onto underwater coral reefs and low sand cays so as to create new islands on which port, airfield and several types of military-related installations are being built.

Further to the north China has initiated numerous air and sea confrontations with Japanese forces in the East China Sea.

Many countries in the Indo-Pacific are disturbed by these developments and are strengthening their deterrence and defensive capabilities.

Meanwhile the US is morphing into a different kind of ally. Many Americans are war-weary, worried by the failure to contain international terrorism, concerned by delays in restoring their economy and frustrated by the fraught processes of decision-making in Washington. There is also deep unease about the assertive behaviour of China, Russia, Iran, North Korea and other authoritarian states and the weakening of many long-standing American technological and military advantages.

In this context, senior American defence and foreign policy thinkers are debating whether they should sustain strong forward commitments, discussing more restrained types of international policy and considering whether they should tolerate allies that fail to pull their weight. The Obama Administration has helped foster this thinking by the hesitancy of its actions in Syria, the broader Middle East and in East Asia, its severely constrained defence spending and its sometimes clumsy management of alliance relations.

Further complicating Australia's strategic outlook is that, in stark contrast to the Cold War, the country is no longer a strategic backwater far removed from the centre of major power tensions. Australia now finds itself close to the centre-stage of global strategic competition and a likely theatre of any future major war. The US, China and a range of other major powers are already manoeuvring to exploit Australia's enhanced strategic significance.

Given these markedly altered circumstances, Australia needs to review its strategic priorities and define a new grand strategy. Australia should strive to secure its vital security interests with a high level of independence. However, the demands of the new strategic environment mean that even multiplying the national defence budget several times over would still leave the country vulnerable to international coercion and several types of serious attack. New sources of security are needed.

This essay argues that Australia should adopt a new grand strategy of partnership and leverage.[1] This grand strategy would focus on four key tasks.

First, Australia should strive to become the indispensable ally of the US in the Indo-Pacific. It should do this by working more closely with American strategic planners and inviting US forces to increase their presence in, and operations from, Australia.

Second, Australia should work hard to become a closer security partner of Indonesia, Japan, South Korea and India.

Third, Australia should develop more valued security relationships with China, Vietnam, Singapore, Malaysia, the Philippines, Papua New Guinea and the countries of the Southwest Pacific.

Fourth, Australia should work to become a more influential player in shaping the Indo-Pacific strategic environment.

Australians must understand the more challenging security environment that is developing and debate their options for action. Australians needs to lift their game.

This essay addresses these issues in the following sequence:

---

1 While discussions of grand strategy are unusual in Australia, there have been some notable contributions on the topic in recent years. They include: Andrew Shearer *Changing Military Dynamics in East Asia: Australia's Evolving Grand Strategy* (Institute on Global Conflict and Cooperation, University of California, January 2012. Accessed at https://escholarship.org/uc/item/5sf691qt on 9 May 2015. Brigadier Wade Stothart, *Navigating Uncertain Times: The Need for an Australian 'Grand Strategy'* (Indo-Pacific Papers, Australian College of Defence and Strategic Studies, Department of Defence, Canberra, March 2015) Accessed at http://www.defence.gov.au/adc/publications/publications.html on 9 May 2015 and Alan Dupont, *Grand Strategy, National Security and the Australian Defence Force* (Lowy Institute for International Policy, Sydney, May 2005) Accessed at http://www.lowyinstitute.org/publications/grand-strategy-national-security-and-australian-defence-force on 9 May 2015.

1. The key characteristics of a successful grand strategy and the evolution of grand strategy in Australia
2. The twelve major changes in the international environment that are driving Australia to re-think its grand strategy.
3. What should be the key goals of a new grand strategy?
4. What foundational judgements should drive the structure of a new Australian grand strategy?
5. What are the options for a new grand strategy and what is preferred?
6. Twelve steps for implementing the proposed grand strategy of partnership and leverage.

Conclusions

1

GRAND STRATEGY AND ITS EVOLUTION IN AUSTRALIA

It is a truism that you are unlikely to get where you want to go unless you have first identified your destination and, second, selected a viable strategy for getting there.

This is the core of grand strategy. It is the game-plan a country selects to progress its primary strategic interests.

A grand strategy should encompass a clear sense of direction, a chosen way of proceeding and also a logic for how a nation's full suite of political, economic, military and other instruments can best be brought to bear to achieve priority strategic goals.

Military historian, Basil Liddell-Hart, described the role of grand strategy as:

> ... – higher strategy – ... to coordinate and direct all the resources of a nation, or band of nations, towards the attainment of the political object of the war – the goal defined by fundamental policy.
>
> Grand strategy should both calculate and develop the economic resources and manpower of nations in order to sustain the fighting services. Also the moral resources – for

to foster the people's willing spirit is often as important as to possess the more concrete forms of power.[2]

More recently, Barry Posen applied a slightly different focus:

> A grand strategy is a nation-state's theory about how to produce security for itself. Grand strategy focuses on military threats, because these are the most dangerous, and military remedies because these are the most costly. Security has traditionally encompassed the preservation of sovereignty, safety, territorial integrity, and power position – the last being the necessary means to the first three. States have traditionally been quite willing to risk the safety of their people to protect sovereignty, territorial integrity, and power position.
>
> A grand strategy enumerates and prioritises threats, and potential political and military remedies to threats. Remedies include alliances, intelligence capabilities, military power, and the underlying economic and technological potential on which it is based. The threats of greatest importance arise from other nation-states, especially states of comparable capability, which can pursue their own interests with any means they choose because they are unconstrained by world law or world government or world police. Though we have seen that private organisations can do great harm through terrorism, their capacity pales against the potential of other nation-states.[3]

These divergent approaches highlight a serious dilemma in developing grand strategy. Liddell Hart argues it must take account of the full resources of a nation, its people, economic capabilities, political skills, military capacities and moral suasion. Posen, on the

---

2 Liddell Hart, B. H. *Strategy: The Indirect Approach* (Faber and Faber Limited, London, 1967) pp. 335-336.
3 Posen, Barry R. *Restraint: A New Foundation for US Grand Strategy* (Cornell University Press, Ithica and London, 2014) p. 1.

other hand, argues grand strategy should focus more narrowly on military threats, because these are the most dangerous, and on military remedies because these are the most expensive.

In Australia's case it is difficult to avoid considering broader economic, human and political factors because these are likely to play important roles in any future foreign coercion or attacks. Moreover, Australia's options for countering coercion and future attacks are likely to include the use of economic and other non-military instruments. For the purposes of this essay, the broader economic, foreign policy and other factors will only be discussed where they are directly relevant to Australia's future security.

Posen argues convincingly that grand strategy has four primary purposes.[4]

First, as available resources are finite, a grand strategy should guide choices about what things are bought to deal with future security challenges and also spending on current and near-term activities. Posen argues it is generally best for a nation-state to be strongest in those fields that really matter, rather than attempting to do almost everything but with weak capabilities that don't perform priority tasks well.

Second, grand strategy provides guidance to the numerous government organisations and private sector entities that need to synchronise their activities in peace and war. In this sense, grand strategy represents the strategic tune that the conductor controls so that all elements of national power contribute the right things at the right time. Hence, effective grand strategy needs to be simply expressed, frequently explained and readily understood by all players in the national security orchestra.

---

4 Posen, Barry R. *Restraint*, pp. 4-5.

Third, grand strategy communicates security intent to international friends and potential foes. Effective grand strategy, when backed by appropriate investments and activities, can reassure allies and friends, persuade neutral or undecided parties, caution competitors and deter potential enemies. Effective grand strategy can hence help shape the international environment and reduce the potential for misperception and miscalculation.

Fourth, grand strategy helps discipline decision-makers to stay on the government's chosen national security path.

Since European settlement Australia has progressed through three grand strategy eras.

Grand Strategy 1: 1788-1942 – Empire Security

When the First Fleet arrived from Britain in 1788 the settlers worked hard to establish a colony that could be fed, sheltered and generate the essentials to sustain itself. They also needed protection from Aboriginal raids and attacks by colonial rivals. As almost all of the settlers were British, they considered it natural to rely for security on the Far Eastern Squadron of the Royal Navy and the local British Army garrison.

The early colonists appreciated that their security depended on Britain staying strong. Hence, when the Empire was seriously challenged in foreign theatres, the Australian colonies contributed military units to fight alongside British forces to help sustain the alliance's strength and as a genuine act of loyalty. It was in this spirit that Australian forces were sent to the land wars in New Zealand, the war in the Sudan, the Boxer Rebellion, the Boer War and the First World War.

Australia's grand strategy for the country's first 150 years sought security and prosperity within the British Empire.

Grand Strategy 2: 1942-1972 – Alliance Security

In early 1942, with the obvious British weakness in Southeast Asia and the looming threat of Japanese invasion, Prime Minister John Curtin turned to the US as the primary guarantor of Australian security. The strength and speed of the US response appeared to validate the very high value successive Australian governments had placed on its allies to guarantee the nation's ultimate security. More than one million Americans served in Australia during this conflict.

But while the identity of Australia's major power partner changed during the Second World War, the alliance strategy itself remained largely intact. Australian governments continued to assume the country could not be defended independently. They relied heavily on a powerful, like-minded ally and they continued to contribute in a range of ways to both defend and strengthen the alliance. A foundational assumption was that should Australia ever be threatened seriously, the major ally would move rapidly to help.

In this spirit, following the Second World War Australian military commitments were made to the occupation force in Japan, to United Nations operations in Korea, to help defend Malaysia and Singapore against Indonesian confrontation and to fight in Vietnam. This active support of American and British operations in Asia came to be known as 'forward defence' commitments.

Grand Strategy 3: 1973-2015 – Defence of Australia within an Alliance Framework

In the 1960s this established alliance framework came under strategic and financial stress. By the late 1970s the British had withdrawn most of their forces from east of Suez and the US had withdrawn from mainland Southeast Asia. Primarily because of this markedly altered strategic environment, in 1973 the Australian Cabinet approved four significantly different priorities for Australian defence planning:

- The direct defence of Australia against credible contingencies with a high level of independence. (This was to be the first priority for defence force development.)
- The fostering of a positive international security environment, especially in Southeast Asia and the Southwest Pacific.
- The maintenance of Australia's close alliance partnerships, especially with the US and New Zealand.
- Fostering the further development of a favourable international order by encouraging adherence to international law, contributing to United Nations diplomatic, peacekeeping and other operations, etc.[5]

For the first time since 1941-44 the direct defence of Australia was to drive Australian defence and security *investments*. Offshore operations with allies and friends were still anticipated and, indeed, were to be accorded some priority in *force activities*. But, in contrast to the past, distant offshore operations were not to drive the design and development of the defence force.

In the decades that followed, Australia's capabilities for the direct defence of the nation were strengthened. However, successive

---

5 For details of the official judgements made at the time see: Stephan Fröhling *A History of Australian Strategic Policy Since 1945* (Defence Publishing Service, Canberra, 2009). See, in particular, pp. 467-485 and pp. 607-623.

Australian governments also committed forces to allied operations in Somalia, Iraq, the Persian Gulf, Timor-Leste and Afghanistan. Australia also accepted an informal leadership role in reinforcing allied security interests in the South Pacific and in key parts of Southeast Asia.

Australia's grand strategy in 1973-2015 was periodically labelled *Defence of Australia within an Alliance Framework.*

Conclusions

Throughout its history, three enduring features marked Australia's grand strategy. First, Australians have always doubted they could defend themselves against a major threat solely with their own resources. Second, Australians have relied on a friendly great power to carry a substantial part of their security burden. And third, Australia has had an enduring interest in helping to maintain a Western-driven rules-based international economic and security order.

2

TWELVE DRIVERS OF A NEW GRAND STRATEGY

Many of the factors that had provided extended continuity to Australia's grand strategy since the early 1970s are under pressure. Australia is now confronted by an international environment that has changed in at least twelve major ways. Consequently, many of the assumptions that long underpinned the country's strategic game-plan need review.

Change Driver 1: China's rising economy

The US and its close allies no longer dominate economic activity in the Western Pacific.

In real, or purchase power parity, terms China's economy is already about the same size as that of the US China certainly faces major challenges in coming years, especially in shifting its orientation from export-led growth to growth driven primarily by domestic consumption. This, together with the maturing of industrialisation and an ageing of the population, means average economic growth rates are likely to be lower. Nevertheless, for the next three decades the pace of economic expansion in China is likely to be faster than that of North America, perhaps twice as fast.

At the same time, China is developing a high level of economic integration with its Western Pacific neighbours. China is already the largest trading partner of Australia, Japan, South Korea and Taiwan and by 2020 will probably be the largest trading partner of every western Pacific rim nation.

For Australia, the strategic implications of China's growth are complex. Some commentators conclude Australia is being inexorably drawn into China's strategic orbit. A few argue Australia should, as a consequence, distance itself from the US.[6] This line of thinking oversimplifies the developing situation and, in particular, overlooks the qualitative aspects of Australia's relationships with its economic partners.

While China is easily Australia's largest trading partner, the figures for merchandise trade, on their own, convey a misleading picture of the economic relationship. China and Australia sell each other large quantities of goods but they trade much lower quantities of services. Indeed, Australia and the US trade more than double the value of services Australia and China exchange.

Perhaps even more revealing, China is only the ninth largest investor in Australia, far behind the US, the UK, Japan and several other European and Asian countries. China, meanwhile, attracts only 1.1 per cent of Australia's investment abroad, compared to 29.8 per cent going to European Union countries and 28.5 per cent going to the US.

There are also major differences in the quality of Chinese

---

6 For a discussion on these and related issues see: Hugh White *Power Shift: Australia's Future Between Washington and Beijing* (Quarterly Essay, Issue 39, 2010).

investments in Australia compared to those from other advanced economies. Many American, European and Japanese investments comprise medium and high technology footprints that contribute to Australia's and the globe's longer-term development and production of cutting-edge systems.[7] By contrast, China's much smaller scale investments in Australia involve very little advanced technology transfer and focus heavily on mineral developments and associated infrastructure together with some residential and agricultural property.

This more complete picture highlights the fact that in many respects the Australia-China economic relationship is conducted at arms-length. The two countries are reluctant to engage intimately in each other's economies by operating extensively in their partner's services sectors and investing in advanced systems. To some extent, this reflects a failure to identify attractive investment opportunities. However, other factors include difficulties in bridging cultural differences, concerns about each other's regulatory, legal and political frameworks and limited levels of trust.

From an Australian perspective, China is certainly rising to be a major economic power. However, because China's economic relationships with Australia and a range of other regional countries largely comprise the simple trade of commodities and manufactured components, Beijing's strategic influence is not as strong as many assume.

---

7 For instance, Boeing's operations in Australia are only second in scale to those in the US Similarly, BAE Systems, Thales, Saab and other global companies in Australia develop and produce advanced technologies and systems to meet worldwide demands. There are other cutting-edge Western investments in Australia's information technology, telecommunications, pharmaceutical industries and other sectors.

Change Driver 2: China's assertive strategy

For Australia and other Western countries the most concerning aspect of China's challenge springs not from the growing strength of its economy, geographic size, vast population or even rising military capabilities. Rather, it springs from the nature of China's authoritarian regime, its Leninist ideology and, most of all, from its assertive and highly revisionist international strategy. China is ruled by a regime that seeks to overthrow large parts of the rules-based international order, created and long nurtured by the Western powers.

The Chinese regime's primary goal is to reinforce the strength and longevity of the ruling Communist Party of China (CPC). That goal is central to the regime's elaborate mechanisms to ensure domestic stability, economic growth and restoration of Chinese pre-eminence in the Indo-Pacific.

The Chinese leadership's strategy has four major sub-goals.

First, China wishes to control information flows to maintain internal cohesion and undermine potential domestic and international opponents. Specific measures include propaganda campaigns to underline the legitimacy of the CPC. Domestic intelligence and cyber operations are conducted to suppress potentially subversive information flows and to identify, monitor, coerce and, when appropriate, arrest dissidents and troublesome minorities. Programs to control information from international sources include very active diplomacy, sophisticated propaganda programs and foreign intelligence operations to, among other purposes, cultivate agents of influence and spread disinformation. These programs also include the propagation of highly assertive legal positions in so-called 'law-war' operations to bolster the legitimacy of Chinese claims. Chinese students and other citizens abroad, together with Confucius Institutes[8] and similar organisations, are periodically marshalled to support Beijing's international operations.

A second goal is to sustain economic growth and modernisation. Sometimes Chinese financial institutions and corporations are encouraged to operate in locations and for purposes that are driven more by the CPC's strategic goals than by intrinsic economic value. China's state-owned enterprises are used in some environments to directly serve Party and national interests by engaging in intelligence and other types of strategic operations.

China's intelligence organisations are heavily engaged in industrial espionage to steal the intellectual property required

---

8 Confucius Institutes have been established in many Western universities, including nine in Australia. These organisations are funded by, and closely affiliated with, the Chinese Ministry of Education. The publicly stated purpose of these Confucius Institutes is "to promote a better understanding of Chinese culture." However the executives of the central headquarters of the organisation in Beijing are all Chinese Government officials and most, if not all, appear to be members of the CPC. Serious allegations have been made about the involvement of Confucius Institutes in espionage and other intelligence-related activities. See, for instance, 'Former Canadian Intelligence Agent: The Confucius Institute Is an Espionage Institution' (NTD.TV, 2 November 2014) http://www.ntd.tv/en/programs/news-politics/china-forbidden-news/20141029/242027--former-canadian-intelligence-agent-the-confucius-institute-is-an-espionage-institution-.html#sthash.IeNtZsnk.dpuf : http://www.ntd.tv/en/programs/news-politics/china-forbidden-news/20141029/242027--former-canadian-intelligence-agent-the-confucius-institute-is-an-espionage-institution-html (Accessed on 7 May 2015). For a critical report on the political role of Confucius Institutes see: Peter Foster 'US professors urge Western universities to end ties to China's Confucius Institutes' *The Telegraph* (London, 7 May 2015) http://www.telegraph.co.uk/news/worldnews/asia/china/10907971/US-professors-urge-Western-universities-to-end-ties-to-Chinas-Confucius-Institutes.html (Accessed on 7 May 2015).

to produce advanced products and services. These operations facilitate Chinese industrial short-cuts and strengthen competitive advantages.

A third important sub-goal is to build strong military capabilities. These are not intended to match those of the US and its allies' ship-for-ship, aircraft-for-aircraft or tank-for-tank. Rather, they are structured asymmetrically to conduct surprise, very fast-paced operations to blind and destroy most traditionally-structured enemy forces that are forward-based in the Western Pacific, while deterring nuclear escalation. To support this development of modern military capabilities, China's intelligence, cyber and military industries are tasked with gathering, assessing and exploiting advanced technologies and military systems so China can outflank or surpass Western capabilities in priority fields.

A fourth key sub-goal is assertive multi-dimensional operations that lay claim to territory, seabed, airspace and parts of outer space that are either poorly defended or difficult for opposing forces to occupy or protect. Through a series of incremental steps by a diverse range of civilian and military agencies, China seeks to create new 'facts' and new 'realities' which are hard for opposing forces to contest. In some cases, such as Chinese operations to undermine Philippine and Vietnamese holdings in the South China Sea, China has been prepared to deploy overwhelming force to coerce acquiescence. In others, such as the harassment of US and Japanese ships and aircraft in the East and South China seas, Beijing has modulated its assertive actions so that they always fall below the threshold for triggering forceful allied responses. The end result is a form of flexible 'salami-slicing' strategy that has gradually expanded China's presence in internationally contested areas and strengthened Beijing's assertion of regional pre-eminence.

The success of these carefully tailored actions has deepened the concerns of East and Southeast Asian governments about China's future goals and it has also undermined regional confidence in the deterrence and defensive value of security partnerships with the US.

Of key importance to the Communist Party's leadership is that these assertive international operations are warmly welcomed at home. They reinforce deep-seated nationalist sentiments and signify progress towards China taking its 'rightful place' as a leading global power.

While there is broad support in the CPC for the four main themes in Chinese strategy, there are signs of disenchantment within the Party concerning some stances taken by its leadership in recent years. In particular, there are concerns about corrupt behaviour and worries about excesses in some counter-corruption campaigns. Many Party members in business also worry about the direction of the economy and difficulties in maintaining economic momentum and social harmony.

When considering the future of China in the coming 30 years, there are three credible categories of scenario:

- First, the CPC leadership may maintain a substantial degree of economic, social and security stability, permitting China to continue its military modernisation and assertive strategic operations. This is most likely.
- Second, the CPC leadership may fear it is losing control of the Party and the country and decide to reinforce its legitimacy and authority by adopting a more nationalist stance. This might lead to more aggressive international operations to rally the population and strengthen national cohesion.

- Third, worsening economic conditions combined with serious corruption scandals and other problems could trigger mass demonstrations and a strong move within the Party to liberalise China's political system. If sustained, such a change could effectively amount to a new Chinese revolution. New political parties might be legalised and permitted to stand against the CPC in elections. While developments of this kind may improve the prospects for more moderate international policies and actions in the longer term, in the short term they would probably be combined with strong nationalist appeals in order to help hold the country together. While this scenario is possible, it is the least likely during the coming three decades.

The bottom line for Canberra is that any of these broad scenarios would likely exacerbate Australia's security challenges. For the medium term at least, China will continue to be a powerful revisionist state, prepared to contest long-standing international norms. This outlook raises important issues for Australia's immediate strategy but even more serious questions for the type of strategy Australia may need in 2020-2040.

Change Driver 3: China's surging military power

While most countries in the Indo-Pacific are taking steps to modernise their military capabilities, the scale, breadth and speed of China's military expansion is having the strongest impact. For the first time since the Second World War, the US and its close Western allies can no longer assume operational dominance in this theatre.

China's announced defence spending grew by an average inflation-adjusted 9.4 per cent per year in the decade to 2013. In fiscal 2014 China's defence spending grew by 12.2 per cent and it is scheduled to rise by a further 10.2 per cent in 2015.[9] While China's defence spending quadrupled during the last ten years, defence spending in the US grew by a total of only 12 per cent.[10]

Western concerns about Chinese military developments are based on more than the trajectory of Chinese defence expenditure. There are ten key Peoples' Liberation Army (PLA)[11] capabilities whose rapid development and deployment is transforming the military balance in the Western Pacific.

First, China is deploying a new generation of strategic nuclear forces that are more capable and able to survive attack. The

---

9 For details see: Elbridge Colby 'Why China's Growing Defense Budget Matters,' *Real Clear Defense* (9 March 2015) http://www.realcleardefense.com/articles/2015/03/09/why_chinas_growing_defense_budget_matters.html Accessed on 19 March 2015. And also Richard A. Bitzinger 'China's Double-Digit Defense Growth: What it Means for a Peaceful Rise', *Foreign Affairs* (19 March 2015)

10 For details see: Office of Management and Budget *Historical Tables: Budget of the US Government* (Washington DC, Fiscal Year 2013) pp. 54, 55. See also 'Trends in World Military Expenditure, 2013' *SIPRI Fact Sheet* Accessed at: http://books.sipri.org/product_info?c_product_id=476 on 9 May 2015. Please note that many categories of defence-related expenditure are omitted from official Chinese budget statements and seriously underestimate the reality. Amongst the excluded categories are the costs of purchasing foreign weapons and equipment and defence research and development.

11 In general discussion PLA usually refers to all arms of the Chinese military forces. In reality, the Chinese military forces primarily comprise the Peoples Liberation Army Army (PLAA), the Peoples Liberation Army Navy (PLAN), the Peoples Liberation Army Air Force (PLAAF) and the People's Liberation Army Second Artillery Force (PLASAF) that manages the nuclear and strategic missile force.

new inter-continental ballistic missiles (ICBMs) are carried on road and rail-mobile transporters that are shuffled through an extensive network of deep underground tunnels and associated alternative launch sites. There are also four new nuclear-powered ballistic missile-firing submarines (SSBNs) in service, with more under construction. Bomber aircraft armed with long-range cruise missiles supplement this growing strategic arsenal.

Second, the PLA has invested heavily in overlapping surveillance systems that are designed to provide a clear picture of what is happening in China's maritime approaches. This surveillance network includes satellite systems, surface wave and over-the-horizon radars, a sophisticated system of electronic emissions monitoring, high-altitude, long-endurance uninhabited aerial vehicles (UAVs) and a developing network of medium and long-range undersea sonar arrays. This means that, in contrast to previous decades, allied aircraft, ships and submarines operating in much of the Western Pacific will in many circumstances be detected, tracked and potentially targeted.

Third, China is fielding a very large force of cruise and ballistic missiles with the capability to accurately strike targets out to 3,000km whether they are fixed bases or ships at sea.[12] These systems provide a strong capability to attack US and allied bases in the region with little warning, potentially destroying most forward-based military capabilities in the first few hours of a major conflict. A notable feature of Figure 1 is that all of the so-called Second Island Chain in the Western Pacific, including the critical US base

---

12 This large force of Chinese medium range ballistic and cruise missiles has no equivalent in the arsenals of the US and its close allies, largely because they are banned from deploying such systems under the terms of the Intermediate-Range Nuclear Force Treaty. The Chinese are not a party to this agreement.

Figure 1: Range Capabilities of China's Land-Based Conventionally-Armed Missiles and the First and Second Island Chains

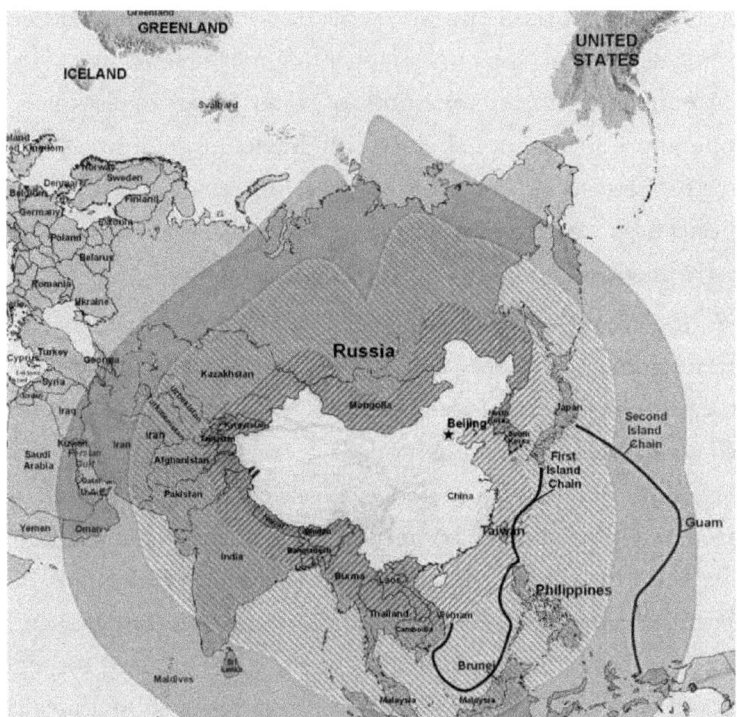

Source: *Military and Security Developments Involving the People's Republic of China 2014* (A Report to Congress Pursuant to the National Defense Authorization Act for Fiscal Year 2000, Office of the Secretary of Defense, Washington DC, 2014) p. 85.

facilities in Japan and Guam, are within range of one or more of these systems.[13]

---

13 In Chinese strategic doctrine the first island chain is normally defined as the area in the Pacific west of a line running from the Kuril Islands south along the Japanese Archipelago, Ryukyu Islands, Taiwan and the northern Philippines to Borneo. The second island chain is generally defined to be the Pacific waters west of a line running from Tokyo, through the Bonin Islands, the Marianas, Guam and Palau to Papua Province in Indonesia. Chinese military doctrine asserts PLA superiority within the first island chain and an aspiration to become dominant within the second island chain.

For Australia, this means the forward-deployed forces of its closest ally in the Western Pacific are more vulnerable to surprise attack than at any time since the Second World War. This brittleness in the allied force posture is encouraging significant revisions to American basing, to patterns of operational deployment, to cooperation with regional allies and friends, to priorities for US force modernisation and to allied theatre strategy. However, these American and allied counters have so far been modest in scale, mostly uncoordinated and slow in implementation.

A fourth major change in China's military capability is the commissioning of fleets of modern nuclear and diesel-electric powered submarines. Most of these new boats carry wake-homing and wire-guided torpedoes and also stealthy supersonic cruise missiles, against which defence is exceptionally difficult. The currently deployed force comprises five nuclear attack submarines (capable of launching torpedoes, cruise missiles and mines), four nuclear powered ballistic missile-firing submarines (SSBN's) and 57 diesel attack submarines most of which carry modern torpedoes and anti-ship missiles. China now operates more submarines than the US and is likely to have between 85 and 100 modern boats in 2030.

A fifth major development is the design, testing and production of several classes of modern warships. In each of the last few years China has laid down, launched or commissioned some 60 naval vessels and now routinely launches more warships each year than any other country. Most of the new surface combatants have multi-purpose capabilities and feature wide-area airspace surveillance and control systems, surface-to-air missile systems and long-range anti-ship missiles. In most respects they are comparable to modern Western warships.

Although China does not seek to match the US in all maritime capabilities its first aircraft carrier, the *Liaoning*, together with its J-15 fighter-bomber aircraft, is now providing an initial sea-based air combat capability. Larger aircraft carriers are believed to be under development but it is doubtful that China perceives a need to match the US in this complex and expensive field. Beijing may prefer instead to further strengthen its asymmetric pattern of defence investments (e.g., overlapping wide-area surveillance systems, ballistic and cruise missiles, submarines, sea mines) so as to place at serious risk the more conventionally structured American and allied forces in the Western Pacific.

A sixth major change is the rapid expansion of China's modern fighter-bomber force. Over 600 fourth-generation aircraft (broadly equivalent to Western F-16s and F/A18s) are in service with several fifth generation combat planes in advanced development (approaching the capabilities of the most modern American air-superiority fighters and fighter-bombers, the F-22 and F35). When operating within China's wide-area surveillance system and supported by tanker and airborne early warning and control aircraft, they are capable of posing a threat to allied maritime and air forces anywhere in the Pacific west of the Second Island Chain.

A seventh major change is the strengthening of China's air defences. Chinese surface-to-air missile systems now form a dense network along most of the eastern coast and in the vicinity of high priority facilities inland. This modern and well-protected air defence system poses a major challenge to Western operations.

An eighth major change is China's development of sophisticated capabilities for space warfare. The Chinese high command views the West's heavy dependence on space-based systems as a major vulnerability. Consequently, it is deploying capabilities to interfere with, damage and destroy space-based systems so that by 2020 the PLA will be able to attack spacecraft in all normally-employed orbits through both missile and unconventional means.

A ninth important Chinese military advance is its development of strong cyber capabilities. The Chinese military appreciates the Western allies depend heavily on secure close-to-real-time transmission, interpretation and display of vast streams of digital data sourced from numerous sensors. The Chinese realise that if, in a crisis, they can cut or severely cripple these information flows, the Western military machine would lose much of its strength. Relevant Australian and allied agencies have in recent years reported extensive Chinese probing, intelligence gathering and various forms of attacks on sensitive information and computer networks.

A tenth major change is development of an aggressive Chinese strategy for serious coercion and major conflict in the Indo-Pacific. This new campaign strategy appears to possess five major components.

The first element in China's theatre strategy is the capability to activate diverse military and quasi-military assets at short notice to apply political pressure against a target country or other entity.

The second element is that, if a major conflict is judged likely, Beijing has the option of launching early strikes to blind US and allied surveillance and reconnaissance systems and destroy or seriously disrupt allied command, control and communications systems.

The third element of China's more aggressive theatre strategy comprises ballistic and cruise missile strikes, air attacks and special force raids to inflict severe damage on U.S, Japanese and other forward-deployed allied forces and their bases. Key targets would include the priority military and logistic support facilities on Guam, the Japanese islands and possibly some support assets in Singapore. The PLA's strategy for major crises is to pre-emptively destroy the US' and allies' primary military capabilities in the Western Pacific and then deliver periodic follow-up attacks so as to prevent facility or force restitution.

A fourth element of China's theatre strategy is to launch strikes on the major naval vessels in this theatre via long range ballistic and cruise missile strikes, submarine attacks and stand-off air strikes.[14] The PLA would aim to secure the waters inside the Second Island Chain from major allied forces.

A fifth element of China's developing theatre strategy is for some PLA units to operate at longer ranges to attack follow-on and logistic support forces in Hawaii, Alaska, on the US West Coast and also in base and staging facilities in Singapore, Australia and Diego Garcia. Submarine, mining and special force operations can be anticipated to destroy, damage or disrupt allied follow-on forces close to their bases or as they transit straits and other choke points. As well as delaying or preventing a meaningful military response, such long-range PLA operations would force the allies to divert substantial resources to protect military shipping and other assets over many thousands of kilometres.

China's new military capabilities have already had a marked impact on Australia's strategic environment. During the coming 25 years, China's anti-access, area denial capabilities are projected

---

14 Stand-off air strikes are those involving aircraft that can launch homing missiles many kilometres from their targets. Launching guided missiles far from enemy forces generally reduces the vulnerability of the attacking aircraft to enemy air defence systems.

to grow stronger, reach out further and manifest themselves in new ways. Moreover China, in contrast to the U.S, can afford to concentrate almost all of its military investments in the Western Pacific and optimise its coercive power and leverage in this theatre. A key effect is to magnify Beijing's strategic influence and its power to manage future crises in Australia's approaches.

The bottom line is that the challenge posed by the PLA to the US and its close allies in the Western Pacific is arguably the most serious Australia has faced since the Second World War. Many of the assumptions that underpinned Australian security planning during the last 70 years are now doubtful. For example, it can no longer be assumed that in this theatre the allies will enjoy an operational sanctuary in space, that their surveillance and information networks will remain inviolate, that their operational bases will have high levels of security or that their air, surface and sub-surface forces will possess uncontested access to the Western Pacific.

These developments in Chinese military strategy and capabilities have fundamental implications for Australia's future defence planning.

Change Driver 4: Geo-strategic switch puts Australia close to centre stage

For the first time in 70 years, Australia now finds itself located near the centre of major power competition.

During the Cold War the primary focus of superpower tensions was Central Europe. This meant that when the Australia, New Zealand, US alliance (ANZUS) was developing its substantive form, Australia was located on the other side of the world from the main action. Australia was in a backwater, able to assist in some marginal ways but never required or able to play a central role in Western strategy.

However, for Australia the long era of comfortable detachment from the centre of global competition is now over. China appears intent on pushing US and allied influence out of East and Southeast Asia in order to restore the regional predominance that most Chinese see as their manifest destiny. China's assertive stance has triggered the US to respond by rebalancing its global posture so that some 60 per cent of US Navy, Marine and Air Force units and over 100,000 US Army troops will be deployed to the Asia-Pacific by 2020.[15] For the first time since the Second World War, Australia's approaches would most likely be the focus of hostilities at the outbreak of conflict between the major powers.

This geo-strategic switch has many consequences for Australia's grand strategy. Australia is no longer a marginal player in superpower contingency planning. In US assessments Australia now looms as a geographically large, strategically located and militarily capable close ally near the centre of future major power hostilities. Not surprisingly, American defence planners are starting to view Australia in a completely different light, reminiscent in some respects of the critical phases of the Second World War.

Change Driver 5: The changing military balance in the broader Indo-Pacific

Partly in response to China's surging strategic capabilities and its assertive international behaviour, Russia, India and Indonesia,

---

15 See: *Deputy Secretary of Defense Robert Work on the Asia-Pacific Rebalance: A Conversation with Robert Work* (Council on Foreign Relations, Washington DC, 30 September 2014), p. 8. Accessed at: http://www.cfr.org/defense-and-security-/deputy-secretary-defense-robert-work-asis-pacific on 20 February 2015.

along with many other Indo-Pacific countries, are modernising and expanding their armed forces.

India

In recent years India's strategic goals have expanded. While Delhi remains concerned to effectively deter and, if necessary, defeat Pakistan, its military development is now driven more strongly by the need to counter the rising military power of China. India has deployed 120 medium range ballistic missiles and some 30 short range ballistic missiles. It is also testing the country's first intercontinental ballistic missile, its first submarine-launched ballistic missile and its first land attack cruise missile. All of these systems will be capable of delivering nuclear weapons.

The Indian Navy has ordered two locally built aircraft carriers, it has active programs to construct both nuclear and conventionally powered submarines and it is also building several classes of destroyers and frigates.

The Indian Air Force plans to upgrade or replace the bulk of its combat aircraft during the coming decade. The Indian Army is modernising its armour, air defence and other systems for high intensity warfare while simultaneously deploying units to contain low-level insurgencies in several parts of the country.

While India's program of military modernisation is impressive, most projects are delayed and there are cost over-runs. Ponderous decision-making and industrial inefficiencies mean that not all of the capabilities ordered will be in service until the late 2020s.

Russia

Russia is also replacing many of its Cold War military systems. Defence expenditure has risen to around 4 per cent of

GDP, breathing new life into some of the country's defence industries.[16]

Moscow plans to replace almost all its land and sea-based strategic missile forces by 2021. The Russian Navy is working to modernise its shore-based infrastructure while simultaneously introducing into service new classes of nuclear-powered submarines and warships. The Russian Air Force is focussing on modernising its command and control systems, improving its combat aircraft fleet and acquiring new types of air-launched weaponry. The Russian Army has been reorganised to provide more high-readiness units and is receiving some new equipment.

Russia remains a major strategic player in the Western Pacific with some 21 submarines and nine cruisers and destroyers, significant numbers of combat and reconnaissance aircraft and four army groups deployed to this theatre.

Indonesia

Indonesia is showing early signs of becoming a more significant player in Indo-Pacific security. During the election campaign and following his installation as president in July 2014, Joko Widodo has talked repeatedly about Indonesia's future maritime role and his desire for the country to be transformed into a 'global maritime axis', with greatly strengthened civil and military maritime capabilities in both Southeast Asia and the Indian Ocean. President Widodo also proposed expanding national defence spending from 0.9 per cent to 1.5 per cent of GDP.

---

16 The draft budget for defence submitted to the State Duma for 2015 was for 4.2% of GDP. For a detailed discussion see: *The Military Balance 2015* (International Institute for Strategic Studies and Routledge, London, 2015) pp. 164-167.

Indonesian officials not only appreciate the strategic importance of the archipelago's international straits but they are also deeply concerned about China's assertion of sovereignty over at least some of Indonesia's Natuna Islands, towards the southern end of the South China Sea. There is a sense that in order to maintain the country's territorial integrity and further its broader strategic aspirations, modernised maritime capabilities deserve priority.

To these ends, Indonesia is buying three new submarines from South Korea, it has bought two light frigates from Britain and another two are being built in Indonesia to a Dutch modular design. The Indonesian Air Force has received 24 refurbished F-16C/D fighters from the U.S, six extra Su-30 fighter-bombers from Russia, new jet trainers from South Korea and a squadron of C-130H transport aircraft from the US and Australia.

In the face of the more challenging strategic environment, Japan, South Korea and many of the ASEAN countries are also upgrading their military capabilities. In most cases they are placing a high priority on bolstering maritime and air defences with some, such as Japan and South Korea, also developing defences against ballistic missile attack.

Change Driver 6: Australia becomes a strategic hinge and anchor

A sixth major change is that both the US and China now view Australia as having significantly greater strategic importance.

In the U.S, Australia is viewed as a large, stable ally that possesses many strategically important characteristics. It has the world's fourteenth largest economy and a well-educated and friendly population. Australia is a fast-rising source of global energy, being the world's second largest exporter of coal. It holds 30 per cent of the world's uranium resources and it will probably be the world's largest exporter of LNG by 2020. Australia is also an increasingly important supplier of food to many Asian countries.

In addition, Australia is a respected and active player in Indo-Pacific affairs and possesses considerable 'soft power' as a result. Institutional, professional and personal linkages across the region are extensive. Some three quarters of the more than half a million international students studying in Australia each year are from Asia.[17] Almost two-thirds of the seven million tourists who visit Australia each year are from Indo-Pacific countries.[18] Several strategically important countries in Southeast Asia and the Southwest Pacific regard Australia as their closest and most trusted political and security partner. Senior Americans realise that these and other factors provide Australia with considerable political leverage in a region whose societies are rapidly modernising.

Allied defence planners also appreciate that Australia has a long track record of being prepared to contribute well-equipped forces to operate in close partnership with American and regional forces on a wide range of priority tasks. The country is viewed as a significant contributor to, rather than a consumer of, regional security.

When American defence planners consider Australia's continental mass, its location close to Southeast Asia and its sophisticated repair and maintenance facilities, they generally conclude the country is an attractive military operating, staging and logistic base.

---

17 For details see: *Studies in Australia – International Students Guide* @ http://www.studiesinaustralia.com/studying-in-australia/why-study-in-australia/international-students-in-australia on 24 March 2015.
18 For details see: Tourism Australia *Visitor Arrivals Data* @ http://www.tourism.australia.com/statistics/arrivals.aspx on 24 March 2015.

Its vast size provides scope for an unusual degree of dispersion and operational flexibility. Australia is currently beyond the reach of a substantial proportion of the Chinese and North Korean missile and air forces but it still provides ready access to many of the operating areas that are likely to be critical in any major power clash in this theatre.

When US forces travel to Australia across the Pacific from the East or across the Indian Ocean from the West, their movement takes place through relatively secure sea and air space. Thus, in a sense, Australia can be described as a strategic hinge, which offers a close-to-ideal environment for staging major military operations into both the Indian Ocean and much of the Western Pacific. It also facilitates the rapid switching of forces between these theatres.

China sees Australia as a major supplier of strategic minerals, several types of energy and quality foods. But when Beijing looks south, it also sees Australia as a major base and concentration area for US military units and potentially other allied forces operating in the Pacific and Indian Oceans.

In addition, Beijing appreciates Australia has unusually close links with several countries in Southeast Asia, in particular Singapore, Malaysia, Indonesia and Thailand. These close ties and frequent military and broader security interactions permit Australian forces to operate into and through the facilities of these regional partners with little formality. This places Australia in an unusually strong position to work in close partnership with key countries in Southeast Asia were there to be a need to bolster their defences, to reinforce their logistic capabilities or to increase security in the region's international straits or air space. In this sense, Australia is seen in China as a large, resource-rich, relatively well-protected anchor for Southeast Asia's security.

Change Driver 7: The rising potential for miscalculation and rapid conflict escalation

A seventh major change in Australia's strategic environment is the significantly increased risk of security miscalculation and conflict escalation in the Western Pacific.

There are two potential causes of miscalculation. First, there is scope for key personnel on each side to misperceive the other side's intentions, plans and actions. This is partly a consequence of a lack of transparency, limited opportunities for meaningful interaction between key personalities and shallow levels of mutual understanding. Consequently, there is scope for serious misperceptions to develop that could lead to dangerous decisions in crises.

A second potential cause of miscalculation in the Western Pacific is sudden aggressive behaviour by operating units. This is intrinsically dangerous and has the potential to be viewed as portending more serious offensive action. China's leadership can readily turn up the 'fervour dial' via the Party-controlled media and directives to deployed PLA units to react strongly whenever they have an opportunity to manoeuvre close to US, Japanese or other allied forces. Notable recent examples of this type of behaviour include exceptionally close aircraft manoeuvres, ships cutting across the bows of rivals to force emergency defensive measures and 'lighting up' ship or aircraft fire control radar systems in a manner that usually precedes the firing of major weaponry.[19] These types

---

19 For details of these types of incidents, see: Ross Babbage *Australia's Strategic Edge in 2030* (Kokoda Foundation Paper No.15, Kokoda Foundation, Canberra, 2011) pp. 28-30, Leszek Buszynski and Christopher B. Roberts *The South China Sea Maritime Dispute* (Routledge, London 2014) and 'US Accuses China Fighter of Reckless Mid-Air Intercept' *BBC News* (23 August 2014) Accessed at: http://www.bbc.com/news/world-asia-china-28905504 on 9 May 2015.

of activity can test the boundaries of the other side's tolerance. They can also trigger major international incidents and potentially stimulate serious retaliatory action.

One of the primary reasons why these dangerous and often provocative actions occur is that limited progress has been made in concluding agreements that define the boundaries of acceptable behaviour. During the early stages of the Cold War, there were numerous similar incidents between the two sides' aircraft, ships and other assets and it took some years before agreements could be negotiated to codify acceptable behaviour when units operate in close proximity. While presidents Obama and Xi Jinping agreed in November 2014 to negotiate similar protocols to avoid dangerous incidents between their respective forces, it is taking time for the details to be settled and applied routinely by forces on operations.[20]

A closely related characteristic of the Western Pacific security environment is the potential for a minor exchange of fire or other provocation to escalate rapidly into major war. This disturbing situation results from the exceptionally strong missile and other offensive capabilities of the new PLA and the concentration and unprotected nature, and hence vulnerability, of key elements of both sides' operating infrastructures. This mutual vulnerability gives both sides strong incentives to strike first and with great force.

In effect, if one side believes major conflict is inevitable and imminent, it will also know that by striking immediately it will decisively win the first major battles.

---

20 For details see: Bonnie Glasser and Jacqueline Vitello 'Summit Provides Momentum for Better Ties' *Comparative Connections* (January 2015) pp. 6-8. http//csis.org/files/publication/1403qus_china.pdf Accessessed on 15 June 2015.

This danger can be illustrated most clearly by pointing out that there are very few major US military bases in the Western Pacific. In normal circumstances the primary American naval and air assets in theatre are concentrated at a small number of facilities in Japan and in Guam. Worse still, very few have hardened structures that would protect allied aircraft and ships from surprise missile or aircraft attack.

If the Chinese high command concludes major war is imminent, it has the power to destroy or seriously damage most American combat forces in the theatre within hours. This would inevitably cause extensive US and allied casualties, limit allied options for early retaliation and, for at least some months, give Chinese forces a predominant position in the theatre.

The dangers of permitting this strategically unstable situation to continue are obvious. Australia can significantly reduce them by assisting the US and its close allies to disperse their forces by providing appropriate alternative bases and other facilities and strengthening logistic and other support resilience in the theatre.

Change Driver 8: New international fluidity brings scope for stronger regional partnerships

The major changes to the Indo-Pacific landscape are not only of concern to Australia. Many other countries are reassessing their strategies and reviewing their security priorities. Several regional countries are considering afresh where they should stand in the strategic competition between China and the US and giving new thought to their future security partnerships. This unusual international fluidity provides important opportunities for Australia, discussed later in this essay.

Change Driver 9: A different United States of America

Another driver for change in Australian grand strategy is that the country's closest ally, the U.S, is morphing into a different sort of superpower. It is entirely possible that the US may emerge in the coming two decades to not possess the largest global economy, its military forces may not be so dominant in the Western Pacific and it may choose to be more detached from international security engagements. The development of a US with these sorts of characteristics would be a very significant departure from Australia's experience since the Second World War and require a thorough rethinking of Australian security priorities and strategies.

With many Americans feeling war-weary after extended military commitments to Iraq and Afghanistan, with the challenges posed by international terrorism not contained, with the US economy emerging only slowly from the global financial crisis and with the processes of political decision-making in Washington fraught and sometimes gridlocked, serious debates are underway about the country's future goals and strategies. One of the reasons for this deep questioning of American international policy is the scale of demographic change in the US. With the passing of the Second World War generation, the influx of Hispanic migrants and substantial shifts in social values, the priorities of many Americans are changing and the burden of international activism is being more acutely felt. In effect, the 'liberal hegemonic order' that G. John Ikenberry argues the US has striven to establish since 1945, and which has largely driven US grand strategy in the decades since, is now under serious challenge.[21]

---

21 G. John Ikenberry, *Liberal Leviathan: The Origins, Crisis and Transformation of the American World Order* (Princeton University Press, Princeton, 2011) pp. 2, 169-193.

Those arguing for much more selective US international engagement state that the high-tempo international activism of the last two decades was unnecessary and unsustainable.

Part of the pressure for change comes from a sense that global security leadership is getting much harder. One reason for this is that the military technological lead that American forces have enjoyed for over 70 years is eroding. On Saturday, 31 January 2015, Bob Work, the Deputy Secretary of Defense, delivered an informal conversational presentation in Washington in which he explained this view in greater detail:

> But now to what I really want to talk about, and that it's become very clear to us that our military's long comfortable technological edge – the United States has relied on a technological edge ever since, well even in World War II. We've relied upon it for so long, it's steadily eroding.
>
> Our perceived inability to achieve a power projection over-match, or an over-match in operations, clearly undermines, we think, our ability to deter potential adversaries. And we simply cannot allow that to happen."[22]

Some Americans argue that striving to restore a clear over-match is unnecessary because US security is underpinned by distance from other major powers, with oceanic expanses effectively protecting it from many forms of attack. America continues to be exceptionally wealthy and its economy is relatively self-sufficient. In addition, the US continues to field the most capable conventional forces on the planet and it retains a powerful nuclear deterrent.

Amongst the downsides of maintaining a liberal hegemonic

---

22 *The Third U.S Offset Strategy and its Implications for Partners and Allies* (A speech delivered by Deputy Secretary of Defense, Bob Work, on 28 January 2015).

grand strategy, the critics argue, is that the allies and friends of the US gain more from the strategy than does the US itself. Allies tend to free-ride on the generous military investments and activities of the US by reducing their own defence spending and focussing national security attention on narrow self-defence.[23] By claiming security guarantees from the US allies effectively hold American security prerogatives hostage. Some allies also act recklessly, knowing that if assertive regional behaviour triggers a serious crisis, Washington will have no choice but to marshal forces for the ally's defence. Posen argues Israel has been a serial offender as a reckless ally.[24]

The better approach to US grand strategy, argue Posen and other critics of liberal hegemonic strategy, is to markedly reduce American force commitments in forward theatres, add major conditions to alliance obligations where allies are not pulling their weight and tolerate, even possibly encourage, the development of nuclear weapons by allies and friendly states to reinforce their own security and reduce the extended deterrence burden on Washington.

This alternative grand strategy, which Posen labels Restraint, would also facilitate reform of the US armed forces into a more compact and modern structure designed primarily to dominate the maritime commons. Posen believes these changes would permit the US to cut its defence spending from 4.5 percent to 2.5 percent of GDP.

For close allies of the U.S, the debate about the future direction of American grand strategy introduces a substantial element of risk. The prospect of the long-running liberal hegemonic strategy being replaced by Posen's proposed strategy of Restraint is

---

23 Posen, Barry R. *Restraint*, pp. 35-44. http//www.defense.gov/Speeches/Speech.aspx?SpeechID=1909 Accessed on 18 June 2015.
24 op. cit., pp. 44-48,

probably remote. However, some features of this type of strategy are evident in the Obama administration's approach in recent years. His administration's track record shows far greater hesitancy to commit forces overseas or to use force against state actors, such as Syria and Iran. There have also been significant force and facility reductions in Europe and severe restraints imposed on US defence investments and spending.

The Obama Administration's approach to alliances is also changing. Allies of the US are expected to be active and substantial contributors to global security, not passive consumers. It is incumbent on close allies to demonstrate regularly that they make a significant difference to the US-led alliance in the scale and pattern of their defence spending, their military commitments to trouble spots, their active diplomacy in support of allied interests and by other means.

Australia's future grand strategy needs to be crafted in a way that is workable when the country's major power ally shifts its own security approach. There may be times in coming decades when American administrations appear to be reverting to a form of activist liberal hegemonic strategy. But, equally, there may be times when the US behaves more like a weary titan and chooses to operate in a more detached, hesitant and even isolationist mode. If Australia wishes to retain the status and comfort of an especially close ally, it will need to demonstrate clearly and repeatedly to American administrations of different types why the country deserves special treatment. It will be necessary for Australia to demonstrate exceptional value to the US and, amongst other things, lift its defence spending to a level that, as a percentage of GDP, is closer to that of its major power protector.[25]

---

[25] The US currently spends about 3.8 per cent of its GDP on defence and Australia currently spends about 1.8 per cent.

Change Driver 10: Weakened extended deterrence

One of the long-standing benefits of a close alliance with the US is the American declaratory policy that an attack on an ally is considered equivalent to an attack on the territory of the US. Since the Second World War this concept of extended deterrence has been used to deter military attacks on the Pacific allies and reinforce the strategic significance of their independent defence efforts. It has also been employed within the alliance network to dissuade allies such as Australia, Canada, Japan and South Korea from contemplating the acquisition of independent nuclear forces. Washington has repeatedly assured these allies that a nuclear attack by a belligerent state on their territory would trigger swift nuclear retaliation by the US.

Robert Manning recently described the core logic of extended deterrence as follows:

> Extended deterrence is designed to persuade adversaries not to attack US allies by convincing them that any attack would be unsuccessful and/or would be met with retaliation that causes unacceptable damage. In short, credible extended deterrence is about convincing adversaries that the risks of aggression far outweigh any benefits.[26]

Manning also emphasises that extended deterrence is designed to convince allies of US capability and commitment to defend them. Unfortunately, the credibility of these American assurances has been undermined by a number of developments in recent years.

First, the substantial shift in the 'correlation of forces' in the

---

[26] Robert A. Manning, *The Future of US Extended Deterrence in Asia to 2025* (Brent Scowcroft Center on International Security, The Atlantic Council, Washington DC, 2014) p. 1.

Western Pacific is reducing markedly Washington's freedom of action in this theatre.

Second, the idea that the US would respond to a nuclear attack on an American ally with one or more nuclear retaliatory strikes stretched credibility in the 1980s when Washington had over 12,000 strategic nuclear warheads at its disposal. With the US strategic nuclear capability now reduced to 2,000 warheads and heading for 1,250 or even to 1,000, the prospect that any US administration would use its thinly-spread nuclear arsenal to defend an ally seems even less credible. With several other nuclear weapon states now holding hundreds of nuclear warheads, American strategic flexibility and extended deterrence is significantly weakened.

Third, US international security policy has been characterised in recent years by caution and periodic timidity. This reflects the American public's war weariness and the Obama administration's predilection to let regional actors settle most regional disputes. A further motivation is a strengthened resolve in both the administration and Congress to rein in defence spending and reduce the scale of the country's budget deficit. A key consequence of this more hesitant American posture is to weaken global perceptions of American leadership.

Fourth, encouraged by the changing correlation of forces and American international caution, China, Russia and, to a lesser extent, North Korea have launched a succession of tailored coercive operations against US allies and friends that always fall below the threshold for triggering American nuclear or even conventional force responses. The most notable area of such operations in the Indo-Pacific is in the South China Sea, where Chinese forces of various types have built new islands on underwater coral reefs and undertaken repeated small incursions and provocations. Over several years, they have given substance to the claim that more than 80 percent of these international waters and numerous islets and reefs come under Beijing's sovereignty. China has sought to 'create new facts' and set new international rules in this theatre. Washington has so far responded with expressions of displeasure and occasional aircraft and ship passages through contested areas.

Fifth, China, Russia, Iran, North Korea and other non-democratic states have proven adept at fostering divisions within the US and allied countries by modulating threats and coercive actions on the one hand with apparently reasonable pleas for cooling-off periods, negotiations and even for offers of various types of partnership on the other. A key consequence has been to complicate American foreign policy, reduce the coherence of Washington's security priorities and undermine the resolution of the US to firmly oppose some challenges to its own and its allies' key interests.

These developments, in combination, have serious implications for the hard-nosed judgements Australian security planners need to make about the level of deterrence that membership of the US alliance will confer in the future.

It is difficult to argue the extended deterrence that Australia enjoyed from the 1950s to 1990s remains unaffected by the five categories of change described above. However, because the power of deterrence springs not only from the real strength of US commitments but also from other people's perceptions of them, considerable uncertainty pervades judgements in this field. How much has extended deterrence been weakened? Is the reduced credibility of American extended deterrence permanent or is there some prospect of recovery? Are there actions that Canberra could take that would help restore the credibility and the power of extended deterrence to underpin the future security of Australia and the other Western Pacific allies? These are important issues to be weighed in crafting Australia's future grand strategy.

Change Driver 11: The diffusion of technologies and the rise of non-state actors

Many technologies and systems that just a few years ago were the exclusive preserve of a few nation states are now readily accessible to terrorist groups, criminal syndicates and commercial enterprises. Systems now operated by many non-state actors include advanced surveillance sensors, secure communications networks and numerous types of advanced weapons systems.

Michael Vickers, the Undersecretary for Intelligence in the US Department of Defense, recently pointed out that satellite imagery and advanced cryptography are now readily available to non-state actors, as are many types of biometric technology, providing new means of tracking persons of interest.[27] Some non-state organisations are also active in cyberspace, partly to enable complex networked activities and sometimes to conduct disruption operations. Corporations, criminal organisations and even terrorist groups are periodically contracted by nation states to undertake sensitive intelligence activities, steal valuable intellectual property or launch cyber attacks on special categories of target.

Technology proliferation is also enabling relatively small nation states to acquire carefully selected military capabilities so as to seriously disrupt the normal operations of the armed forces of advanced countries. Amongst these systems are precision strike

---

27 Sydney J. Freedberg Jr '6 Threats, 6 Changes, and a Brave New World' *Defense News – Breaking Defense* (21 January 2015), p. 1.

munitions, robotic surveillance and weapons, counter-space systems and nuclear, chemical and biological weapons. The acquisition of tailored mixes of these systems can make some regions of the world dangerous for even major power forces to enter and they can be very expensive to counter.

In summarising the challenges posed by these developments to the military operations of the US and its close allies, the National Defense Panel Review of the 2014 Quadrennial Defense Review concluded:

> In fact we believe this erosion of America's military-technological advantage is accelerating faster than many defence planners assume. With precision munitions proliferating rapidly, the risks to US military forces are rising in each of the plausible contingencies the Department of Defense uses to assess current and programmed forces. Moreover, the emergence of unmanned and increasingly autonomous systems and other emerging technologies is likely to cause another significant perturbation in military affairs. At least 75 countries are investing in unmanned systems and they are beginning to be employed by actors as diverse as Hezbollah and China. The combination of precision-guided munitions and unmanned and increasingly autonomous systems poses a significant and growing challenge for US defense planners, threatening both our security and global stability. As Secretary Hagel has said, 'we are entering an era where American dominance on the seas, in the skies, and in space can no longer be taken for granted.'[28]

---

28 William J. Perry and John P. Abizaid (co-chairs) *Ensuring a Strong U.S. Defense for the Future – The National Defence Panel Review of the 2014 Quadrennial Defense Review* (advance copy) (United States Institute for Peace, Washington DC, 31 July 2014) p. 21.

Change Driver 12: The emergence of a new global order

The major changes in the international environment highlighted above suggest that we are witnessing the emergence of a new world order. This global order is characterised by new power centres and norms of international behaviour, including abandonment of the use of force as a last resort and disregard for the UN Convention on the Law of the Sea. The new global order is also characterised by areas of major power friction that are markedly different from those of the Cold War or of the subsequent 'unipolar moment'.

In October 2014 the outgoing Secretary of Defense, Chuck Hagel, after pondering the major changes underway in the international security environment said: 'I think we are living through one of these historic, defining times ... We are seeing a new world order – post-World War II, post-Soviet implosion – being built.'[29]

Conclusion

The bottom line of this discussion is that the developing strategic environment is substantially different to that of the last forty years. Australia is now confronted by a strategic context notable for:

- the rise of a powerful China ruled by an authoritarian regime employing an assertive, revisionist international strategy crafted to challenge the US for pre-eminence in the Indo-Pacific;
- Australia being propelled from a strategic backwater to

---

29 Quoted in David A. Graham, 'Defence Secretary Chuck Hagel: Get Used to Endless War', *The Atlantic*, (29 October, 2014). http//www.theatlantic.com/international/archive/2014/10/defense-secretary-chuck-hagel-get-used-to-endless-war/382079/ (Accessed on 18 June 2015).

being located close to the centre stage of superpower tensions and potential major conflict;

- the rise of other major powers and non-state actors bringing greatly increased complexity to international security;
- increased scope for crisis misperceptions and conflict escalation;
- a less confident and less dominant US searching for close allies that can contribute significantly to global security;
- a marked weakening of US extended deterrence;
- many regional countries reviewing their security and providing new opportunities for Australia to foster closer defence and security partnerships; and
- the emergence of a new global order in which many norms of post-war international behaviour are being challenged.

In these changed circumstances any assumption that the security dynamics of the period ahead will be the same as those of the past is flawed. There is a need to take stock of the changed situation, consider carefully alternative grand strategy options and implement an approach that offers the best prospect of protecting Australia's security in the rather different times that lie ahead.

3

GOALS

What precisely should a new grand strategy be designed to achieve? What should the ADF be designed to do and what does it need to acquire?

Successive governments have defined Australia's strategic interests in broadly similar terms. A synthesis of national security statements and defence white papers of the last decade identifies four goals. We must be able to:

- deter and defeat armed attacks on Australia;
- ensure a safe and resilient population;
- contribute to security contingencies in the Indo-Pacific region, with priority given to Southeast Asia and the Southwest Pacific; and
- promote a rules-based international order.

While listing these goals is helpful, it does not make clear which should be accorded highest priority. Nor does it spell out how these goals are to be achieved. Since Australia cannot afford every type of defence capability, hard choices must be made. Once contingency priorities have been established it is relatively easy to determine what should and should not be bought for the defence force and, indeed, for the broader security structure.

The contingencies Australia's force structure should be designed to meet and that should determine acquisitions can be weighed using three key criteria:

- **probability**: what is the likelihood of a particular contingency arising in a way that would require Australian military deployment?
- **consequence:** could the particular contingency category threaten Australia's survival or the lives of its citizens, or is the threat to a lesser interest?

  Australian defence planners generally define *vital* interests to only include defence of the country's sovereign territory and exclusive economic zones at sea, and the security of Australian citizens abroad.

  Non-vital but important security interests include the maintenance of friendly control of the archipelagic screen across Australia's northern approaches and the protection of allied forces, especially those of the US and New Zealand.

  While Australia and its people could be mortally wounded if its vital interests were to be attacked, it could survive some denting from an attack on its non-vital interests.

- **timing:** how quickly could a contingency requiring an Australian military response arise? Could it occur within hours, months or years and what chance would Australia have to detect, assess and acquire relevant capabilities to respond?

Probability, consquence and timing must be weighed against one another if we are to make rational decisions about the contingencies deserving priority and the acquisitions we need to make to match them. We might judge, for example, that it is relatively unlikely that a foreign country would launch a missile, maritime or other direct attack on the Australian continent. Despite its low assessed probability, however, the consequences of such an attack would be serious and, in some circumstances, it could arise quickly.

A serious internal security crisis in a country in the Southwest Pacific, on the other hand, might be considered much more likely to occur. It would not pose a serious threat to Australia's vital interests but it could arise with only a few days or weeks' notice.

A third contingency category might be engaging in nation-building tasks in partnership with allies and friends in the Middle East. This might be assessed as being of high probability but low importance and the timing of Australia's commitment might be non-critical.

The first contingency, coercion or direct attack, would rate very highly for force structure design, primarily because it threatens vital interests and has the potential to arise at short notice. The other contingency categories would not be primary drivers of what is bought for the Defence Force because they do not threaten vital interests. However, should they arise, the government of the day may still decide to respond by committing forces to address them. The key difference is that the structure and design of the ADF would not be driven by the needs of the second and third categories of contingency. However, having bought a force structure primarily to meet contingencies of high consequence that could arise quickly, that same force structure could, and probably would, be deployed to perform other tasks.

Assessing contingencies against probability, consequence and timing would apply rigour to priorities for major defence investments. With discipline it would ensure that Australia's limited defence and national security resources are invested to give the best possible chance of defence in the situations that matter most. This methodology would also help prevent large investments in capabilities only relevant to lower priority contingencies or which are championed by special interest groups.

Applying this proven logic to the markedly different circumstances now developing in the Indo-Pacific does, however, require a serious re-think of the country's grand strategy. The grand strategy of 'Defence of Australia within an alliance framework' that has been in place since the early 1970s has had merit. But it fails to address adequately the challenges and opportunities that now confront the country.

It's time to consider new approaches.

4

Foundational Judgements

To determine the central features of a new grand strategy it is helpful to address eight key questions.

> *1: Can Australia trust non-democratic, authoritarian states to abstain from the threat or use of force in the event of a serious dispute with Australia and/or its allies?*

The short answer is no.

Authoritarian non-democratic states are already threatening and actually using armed force to coerce opponents and rivals. Russia, China and North Korea have engaged in several types of coercive military and para-military operations against other states in recent years.

As some of these countries gain greater economic, military and political power in the decades ahead, there can be no assurance that these behaviours will cease. Consequently it would be prudent for Australian defence planners to assume that some of these countries may threaten, or actually use, military force on a larger scale in the years ahead.

> *2: Is there a credible risk of Australia having to face serious coercion or a military attack in the coming three decades?*

The short answer is yes.

Although there is no immediate prospect of another nation forcibly coercing or attacking Australia, the major shifts in global power, the substantial rise in sophisticated long-range military capabilities in the Indo-Pacific and the more frequent early use of force to settle disputes suggest there is a finite risk of either or both. Such threats might arise from a direct dispute with a foreign power or, alternatively, as a result of a broader struggle between an aggressor and one or more of Australia's allies and friends.

Many forms of coercion or attack are possible. In recent years Australia has been subjected to intensive intelligence, cyber and other foreign operations. In a crisis, threats might be posed to Australia's space and communications assets, maritime and air transport routes and key installations by, for instance, special force raids, air and missile strikes, aggressive cyber attacks, the laying of sea mines and submarine attacks on shipping and coastal installations.

> 3: How should security planners weigh the probability of such threats against their importance for the nation's security and the speed with which they could arise?

While the possibility of serious coercion of Australia or direct military attacks against it remains low, it is probably rising.

Since the Second World War, Australian defence planning has assumed serious coercion or attacks on Australia would most likely spring from a dispute with a neighbour, or as a by-product of conflict between the Soviet Union and the US.

Now, however, Australia faces a much more complicated and unpredictable international environment and the US' primary strategic rival is located in our regional approaches. There is a possibility such a conflict might be triggered by clashes in maritime Southeast Asia or even in Australia's closer approaches. In the event of a conflict erupting between the US and China early attempts to coerce Canberra should be anticipated and parts of Australia would probably be targeted. This is a markedly different strategic equation to the Cold War, when the centre of global rivalry was on the other side of the world.

Should Australia be attacked in coming decades the level of damage could be substantial and sustained for an extended period. Consequently, this category of contingency deserves a high priority in defence planning. The *2013 Defence White Paper* summarised it well:

> Although a direct armed attack on Australia remains unlikely the consequences would be so serious that the possibility must be given priority in our defence planning.[30]

Because of the nature and scale of military modernisation programs across the Indo-Pacific, the capacities of several large countries to launch military operations into Australia's region at short notice are also rising. This means Australian defence planners can no longer assume extended periods of warning and defence preparation time prior to future crises or attacks. Australia needs to be capable of deterring and defending itself against a wider range of credible threats at short notice, either through its own or collective efforts.

> *4: Is it in Australia's interests to see the US-led Western alliance retain its dominance in the Indo-Pacific region?*

The short answer to this question is yes.

---

30 Department of Defence, Defence White Paper 2013 (Commonwealth of Australia, Canberra, 2013) p. 24.

The US-led Western alliance has proven a very effective constraint on anarchic behaviour in the international environment. Any state or non-state actor considering aggressive action against Australia needs to consider the prospect of a forceful response from the US and other allies as well as from Australia. A serious weakening of this Western deterrence and defensive power in the Indo-Pacific would leave Australia more vulnerable to foreign coercion and attacks and require the diversion of much larger resources to ensure the country's security.

Additionally, the US, Britain and their Western allies have fostered a set of international norms and behaviours that have underpinned Australia's security and prosperity since the first European settlement. Australia has gained greatly from the Western-driven liberal rules of trade, international finance, transport, communications and many other areas of interaction and has a strong interest in seeing them maintained.

5: Should Australia seek a closer or a more distant security relationship with the U.S?

Australia has enjoyed a close security relationship with the US since 1917 and an unusually intimate alliance since the US entered the Second World War in 1941. This partnership has provided many security benefits to both parties. The close relationship with the US has long been judged to enhance Australia's deterrence and defensive capabilities in ways other means can't match.

Nevertheless, in recent decades some have argued Australia could better guard its security by distancing itself from Washington. By taking what is sometimes described as a more 'balanced' stance on its future security, it is said that Australia would be less vulnerable in future crises, could ride through them in a semi-neutral position and even contribute to their resolution by serving as an intermediary.³¹

There are serious problems with these arguments at every level. They assume a quasi-neutral Australia would have little interest in seeing the world's liberal democracies retain predominance over, and freedom from, the manipulation of authoritarian revisionist states. It would be naïve to assume that the weaker deterrence and defensive position of a 'balancing' Australia would somehow command the respect of all parties and protect the country from coercion, manipulation or attack.

Advocates of a quasi-neutral stance tend to underestimate the practical difficulties of attempting to acquire and maintain independent security equivalence. Reducing or abandoning the American alliance would undermine Australia's diplomatic clout across the Indo-Pacific, including in Beijing and Washington, reduce substantially Australia's deterrence and defensive power and render the country more vulnerable to foreign manipulation.

Quasi-neutrality would also be out of step with public opinion. Polling indicates 82 per cent of Australians support the security alliance with the US and 61 per cent support the basing of American troops in Australia.³²

With Australia now moving into a period when it will be exposed to more serious security challenges in its approaches and potentially

---

31 See this discussed at some length in Joint Parliamentary Committee on Foreign Affairs and Defence *Australia's Relationship with China – Chapter 5* (Parliament of Australia, Canberra, March 2006). Accessed at: http://www.aph.gov.au/Parliamentary_Business/Committees/Senate/Foreign_Affairs_Defence_and_Trade/Completed_inquiries/2004-07/china/report02/c05 on 9 May 2009.
32 For details see: *Lowy Institute Poll 2013* at: http://www.lowyinstitute.org/publications/lowy-institute-poll-2013 (Accessed on 9 May 2015).

higher levels of security unpredictability, the value of the alliance with the US is not undermined but magnified. If Australians wish to see a continuance of Western security predominance, if they want to further develop strong diplomatic and political links and leverage across the Indo-Pacific and if they wish to have continued access to much higher levels of deterrence and defensive capability than they could ever afford independently, there is a strong case for Australia to further strengthen its alliance with the US.

This will not remove the need for Australian governments to increase their own defence efforts. However, Australia's independent defence and security investments can be undertaken most effectively and at lowest cost and risk within an even closer alliance with the US.

6: Can Australia rely on the United States to respond effectively if Australia's vital interests are threatened by a major power?

The short answer is most of the time.

American defence planners are placing rising value on Australia's geostrategic value as a southern anchor and strategic hinge in the Western Pacific. Australia has long been a close and trusted ally whose defence would be uncontroversial to most Americans. In addition, senior American officials appreciate that Australia has a strong capacity to stir support in the US Congress, in American industry, in the media and in many influential sectors of American society. US officials are also well aware that abandoning a close ally in its hour of need would imperil the entire Western alliance system.

Nevertheless, it is possible to conceive of circumstances when the US may not respond to an Australian security crisis as Canberra would wish. For instance, the two countries may have different priorities, as in the early stages of the 1999 East Timor crisis. It is also conceivable that Australia could come under heavy pressure while the US was distracted by security crises elsewhere, such as in the Middle East.

These risks mean Australian defence planners must invest in the capabilities to independently secure the nation's vital interests. We must improve our intelligence collection and assessment capabilities, our ability to deny hostile military forces access to Australia's approaches and our capabilities to mount counter-coercion operations. These risks also underline the importance of ensuring appropriate levels of energy and food security.

The bottom line is that in nearly every conceivable contingency in which Australia's vital security is at stake, the US could be expected to help. However, Australian planning needs to ensure that if the country has to defend itself for a period with its own resources, it has the wherewithal to do so.

7: Should Australia foster closer security partnerships with key Indo-Pacific nations?

The short answer is yes, definitely.

Australia already has extensive relationships with all key countries in the Indo-Pacific region. However, given the increasingly challenging character of the security environment there is a strong imperative to renew and extend these key connections. Particular priority should be given to strengthening the security partnerships with Indonesia, Japan, China, South Korea, India, Malaysia, Singapore and the Philippines.

Primary goals of enhanced efforts with regional powers should include deepening personal relationships and mutual understanding, strengthening regional security resilience and pursuing new areas of mutually beneficial security cooperation.

8: How much can Australia afford to spend on defence?

Australia is currently spending about 1.8 per cent of Gross Domestic Product (GDP) on defence.[33] This compares to 3.7 per cent for the US, 2.35 per cent for the United Kingdom, 4 per cent for Russia and 2 to 3 per cent for China. The global average spend on defence is 2.11 per cent of GDP.[34]

Across the last decade Australian defence spending has fluctuated between 1.6 per cent and 1.86 per cent of GDP. However, during serious crises Australia has spent much more. Defence spending rose to 4 per cent of GDP during the Vietnam War, 5 per cent in the Korean conflict and at the height of the Second World War it peaked at 32 per cent of GDP.[35]

The current Australian government was elected in 2013 with a promise to spend 2 per cent of GDP on defence within a decade. The previous government's 2013 Defence White Paper also committed to increasing defence funding towards 2 per cent of GDP but cautioned that "this is a long-term objective that will be implemented in an economically responsible manner as and when fiscal circumstances allow".[36]

The level of defence spending ultimately rests upon the depth of public and political concern for the country's security and the state

---

33 Mark Thomson, *The Cost of Defence: ASPI Defence Budget Brief 2014-15* (Australian Strategic Policy Institute, Canberra, 2014) p. 40.

34 For details see: International Institute for Strategic Studies, *The Military Balance 2014* (Routledge, London, 2014) pp. 486-492 and Mark Thomson, *The Cost of Defence: ASPI Budget Brief 2014-15* pp. 161-177. Please note figures for China and Russia are the publicly announced defence budget totals. The real figures are believed to be 30%-60% higher. For details see ISS, *Military Balance 2014*, pp. 209-210.

35 Mark Thomson *The Cost of Defence*, pp. 178-179.

36 Department of Defence, *Defence White Paper 2013* (Commonwealth of Australia, Canberra, 2013) p. 72.

of the national economy. Given Australia is currently suffering the effects of low productivity levels, reduced terms of trade, a reform impasse in the Senate and the prospect of budget deficits for many years to come, extra funding for defence will not be easily won. That said, given effective management of the economy Australia could recover to a buoyant state within five to eight years, making an upward trajectory in defence spending possible.

Alternatively, a major crisis or series of crises in the Indo-Pacific might so concern the Australian people and government that defence spending is boosted rapidly at the expense of other priorities. Nevertheless, it would be prudent to assume that defence spending will remain around the current level for the next five years, with some prospect of a rise to 2 per cent of GDP within a decade.

Conclusion

In addition to pursuing the broad goals of Australian strategic policy mentioned briefly above, this discussion suggests a new grand strategy should be designed to:

- mobilise the full range of Australian political, economic, social and defence resources to help foster a prosperous, confident Indo-Pacific and a liberal rules-based international order;
- provide credible means of deterring and defeating serious political, economic and military coercion;
- provide means of deterring or defeating credible military attacks at short notice;
- maintain and further develop capabilities to conduct the most vital tasks with a high level of independence;

- facilitate a closer strategic relationship with the US and also contribute significantly to the continuance of predominant US deterrence and defensive power in the Indo-Pacific region;
- foster closer defence partnerships with priority states in the Indo-Pacific region; and
- embrace cost-effective approaches that, in the short term, are affordable with defence spending below 2 per cent of GDP.

In addition, any new grand strategy should satisfy the selection criteria for a successful grand strategy that were discussed in Section One. In particular, it should:

- focus resources on dealing with the contingencies that really matter;
- provide clear guidance to all relevant government and non-government organisations;
- communicate intent to international friends and potential foes; and
- discipline decision-makers to stay on the government's chosen security path.

Applying these design criteria to grand strategy options helps assess their respective strengths and weaknesses and leads to some clear conclusions.

5
OPTIONS

Deterrence

While deterrence is an important strategic outcome it has several offensive and defensive types and there are many ways of achieving them.[37] Given this, adopting the concept as a grand strategy would not provide clear guidance to key domestic government and non-government agencies nor to international parties. Further, a strategy of deterrence would also not necessarily require the development of closer defence partnerships with priority states across the Indo-Pacific, including the US.

---

37 There are two main categories of deterrence: offensive and defensive. The core of offensive deterrence is that if A threatens B, B indicates clearly that it can strike back at A so hard that it will not be sensible for A to contemplate attacking B. A clear instance of offensive deterrence was the doctrine of mutual assured destruction employed by both superpowers during the Cold War. The core of defensive deterrence is that if A threatens B, B makes clear to A that by striking B, A will damage its arm so badly that it will regret striking in the first place. Cases of defensive deterrence include the Swiss concept of porcupine defence and the Singaporean concept of the poisoned shrimp. The capability requirements of the two categories of deterrence differ markedly and it is difficult for the broad concept to provide the type of clear guidance that is essential for an effective grand strategy.

Defence of Australia

The defence of Australia is a bedrock objective but using the label to state the country's grand strategy would not provide clear guidance to either domestic or international constituencies. This is largely because the term says little about *how* the country is to be defended. Almost any approach and any investment program could be said to contribute to the defence of Australia. The concept would be an inadequate guide for spending discipline.

In addition, a general concept branded the 'Defence of Australia' provides little sense of whether and how Australia should engage with its regional neighbours or with the US.

Independent defence

The aspiration of providing effective security with a high level of independence is a long-standing theme in Australian strategic thought. The general intent is to ensure Australia maintains its sovereign right to make its own security and defence decisions and is not dependent on others to defend the country in the event of serious threat.

While this concept is driven by laudable sentiment, it carries serious conceptual and practical problems. First, how independent do Australian intelligence assessment, defence planning, capability development, military operations and logistic support need to be in order to secure the country's sovereign rights? The truth is that no country, not even the US, Russia or China has a defence and security system that is completely autonomous. Successive Australian governments have determined it not only makes little sense to attempt such autonomy but it is impractical to try.

Australia currently receives from its close allies privileged access to high-grade raw and processed intelligence, advanced military technologies and systems, the world's most sophisticated training and exercise facilities and many other things besides. Even if Australia multiplied its defence and national security expenditure many times, it would still be impractical to replicate most of these capacities independently. Should Australia cut itself off from allied and friendly sources the reality is that Australia's security would be weakened seriously and the country's international influence undermined.

However, as argued above, there is strong logic in ensuring that in the event that Australia is forced to defend itself for a period with very limited external assistance it can perform the most vital tasks well. This intermediate stance ensures Australia can continue to enjoy all of the advantages of close partnerships with allies and friends while still ensuring the country possesses capacities for independent decision-making and action.

Hedging

Hedging describes one characteristic of a potentially successful grand strategy. A properly designed grand strategy will not only generate immediately deployable capabilities but will also provide a basis for rapidly expanding and/or adapting extant capabilities to deter, defer or defeat whatever security challenges the uncertain international security environment may produce. Hence, a good grand strategy provides a flexible capability to hedge against an unknowable future.

The primary problems with hedging as a basis for grand strategy are that it fails to provide clear guidance about strategic goals and how they are to be achieved. As such it would be a very imprecise measure against which to hold officials accountable. In addition, a grand strategy of hedging fails to provide any guidance to international actors, in particular to close allies and major regional partners.

The preferred option: Partnership and Leverage

Given the inadequacies of the alternative strategies discussed briefly above, this essay proposes a grand strategy that combines two key categories of action: partnership and leverage. This strategy is designed to strengthen security partnerships with allies and regional partners and build Australia's leverage with all key international actors. It is designed to be effective in peacetime, in periods of tension and also in the event of serious conflict.

Partnership

The strategy of partnership and leverage proposes a substantial strengthening of Australia's political, economic, defence and broader security relationships. Priorities would be accorded to close allies, especially the US, the United Kingdom and New Zealand and also to the major regional powers with which Australia has developing security relationships, most notably China, Japan, South Korea and India. In addition, some priority would be given to further developing security cooperation with key regional security partners, particularly Indonesia, Papua New Guinea, Singapore, Malaysia, the Philippines, Vietnam and the island states of the Southwest Pacific.

The primary purposes of these strengthened regional partnerships would be enhanced personal and professional linkages, deeper knowledge and understanding of these countries' security thinking and pursuit of an enhanced range of cooperative security activities.

In Southeast Asia, the South Pacific and the Indian Ocean, a primary focus would be to encourage local states to strengthen their capabilities to resist external interference and coercion. Working closely with the national security leaders of each country, tailored programs of capacity enhancement would be developed. These could include the provision of specialised consulting services, the supply of key technologies or systems, assistance with enhanced education and training and many other activities. Bilateral or multilateral exercising and training with Australian forces would reinforce such activities. Importantly, regional country leaderships should be the primary drivers of what is done in each case.

With the US and other close allies, a primary focus would be facilitating more diverse operations on and from Australian territory. This combined planning, operational and logistic activity would be designed to contribute substantially to development of the allied Offset Strategy[38] for the Indo-Pacific region. Among the benefits would be greatly strengthened allied deterrence, much closer security cooperation amongst regional states and a reinforcement of regional country confidence in their capabilities to resist intimidation.

---

38 The search for a new Offset Strategy, that is currently the focus of much attention in the US, is an effort to develop new concepts and capabilities to neutralise the anti-axis area-denial and other asymmetric strategies currently being employed by a number of revisionist states, including Iran, North Korea and China. This initiative is in its early stages and there are opportunities for close allies to make innovative contributions.

Leverage

The second part of the proposed new grand strategy is that of strengthening Australia's strategic leverage.

First, it is important for Australian security planners to appreciate that for the alliance with the US to remain robust and reliable in the more demanding strategic environment now developing, Australia needs to lift its game.

Canberra should work hard to ensure Australia becomes a far more valuable American ally in the Indo-Pacific.

One upside of the developing strategic environment is that Australia can now employ a broader range of 'currencies' to strengthen the US alliance. For instance, Australia could contribute more to the alliance by lifting its defence spending, it could further strengthen defence force interoperability with the US and it could continue to make helpful contributions to allied operations in more distant theatres. In addition, Canberra could significantly expand its contribution of raw and processed intelligence, extend its sharing of wide-area surveillance data, participate more actively in the development of allied strategies and plans for the Indo-Pacific region and work harder to contribute innovative and very high quality strategic advice to senior US officials.

The Australian Government could also invite the US and other close allies to use a wider range of defence and related facilities in Australia, to strengthen their regional military presence and capacities to conduct contingent operations in the theatre. Australia could also offer to support American forces operating in Australia by providing access to Australia's extensive technological, industrial and broader logistic capabilities.

By reviewing its contributions in all these alliance currencies,

Australia has the potential to become the US' closest ally in the Indo-Pacific and secure an unusual level of influence in Washington. This would deliver numerous benefits including exceptionally close strategic and operational coordination, significant enhancement of Australia's independent military capabilities and a substantial boosting of Australia's deterrence capacity.

Australia should also seek to increase its leverage with a number of major regional powers with which it has developing security relationships, most notably China, Japan, South Korea and India. Cooperation programs would need to be tailored for each of these countries to significantly increase their value for both parties. For instance, with China the emphasis might be on enhanced intelligence and policy dialogues and upgraded exercises to deal with serious counter-terrorism incidents and natural disasters. With Japan and South Korea, the focus might be on deeper policy exchanges, closer surface and sub-surface maritime cooperation and on combined exercise activities in Australia and elsewhere. Periodic Japanese use of Australia's large and relatively unconstrained exercise facilities could be of special value to its Self Defence Force. With India the focus might be on substantially upgraded intelligence and policy exchanges, expanded programs of officer education, some categories of coordinated maritime operations and new types of combined air and maritime exercises.

With each of these countries the aim would be to devise enhanced cooperative measures that add real value to each party and are economically sustainable. Over time, the outcomes would be markedly improved practical security cooperation, strengthened professional and personal relationships between key security decision-makers and enhanced capacities for combined operations.

When possible, habits of combined activity and joint contingency planning should be institutionalised.

With the closer security neighbours in Southeast Asia and the Southwest Pacific, efforts to strengthen security partnerships would need to be tailored even more to local needs. With Indonesia a long menu of options deserves consideration. It could include significantly extended intelligence and policy exchanges, expanded arrangements for officer education, extended avenues of technical and logistic cooperation and further development of combined exercising and training activities. On the other hand, some of Australia's security partners in the Southwest Pacific don't possess a defence force and their primary security requirements are driven by managing offshore fisheries, countering serious and organised crime and protecting their island communities from natural disasters. In each of these countries fresh consultations would be required to clarify priority security needs and discuss where and how Australia could best add value. Most of these partnering activities would be undertaken on a bilateral basis. The overall goals would be to improve the closeness of security cooperation, encourage a strengthening of national resilience and foster personal and professional links so that Australia is seen across the region as a reliable security partner and advisor of first choice.

At its core, the strategy of partnership and leverage would also substantially enhance Australia's deterrence and defensive capabilities against any attempt to coerce or attack the country.

It would do this primarily by inviting the US to make increased use of Australia to support American air, naval and ground force operations. This step would confirm to any potential aggressor that Washington will likely see threats to Australia as threats to the US.

Second, the strategy of partnership and leverage would foster a network of close security partners across the Indo-Pacific which broadly share Australia's security concerns. In the event of external aggression these countries would likely conduct cooperative operations to bolster the region's resilience and defences.

Third, a strategy of partnership and leverage would develop coordinated military and civil capabilities within Australia that, in a situation of major threat, could be mobilised to both protect the country's vital interests and also apply great pressure on a regional opponent to desist. Amongst the options for applying powerful leverage against an aggressive regional power could be the imposition of a distant blockade on the opponent's strategic shipping in close partnership with allies and friends. Another possible option for applying powerful leverage on an aggressive power could be to threaten other key interests of the opposing decision-making elite.

A central aim of the strategy of partnership and leverage would be to ensure any potential opponent of Australia confronted very strong deterrence and defensive capabilities. At its core, the proposed strategy offers powerful leverage to deter regional bullying and force any aggressor to cease operations and quickly come to reasonable terms.

6

Twelve Steps to Implementation

Twelve practical steps provide substance to the proposed strategy of partnership and leverage. If they are taken during the coming two decades, Australia will be far better placed to deal with the more demanding security environment now developing.

1. Regional Security Partnership Program

Australia should launch a regional security partnership program that builds on existing security relationships to further strengthen security understanding, provide assistance to overcome security weaknesses and foster greater security resilience. As discussed briefly above, the program's precise form would depend on the circumstances of each nation, the priorities of the relevant security and defence leadership, and the extent to which Australia is capable of assisting in an effective manner. This initiative would require coordinated whole-of-government action, including by the Department of Foreign Affairs and Trade, the Australian Federal Police, state and territory police, the Department of Immigration and Border Protection, etc.

Over time the intent would be to significantly improve regional confidence and security resilience and encourage key Indo-Pacific and Southwest Pacific security leaders to view Australia as their closest and most responsive security partner.

2. Regional Communications, Command, Control, Computer, Intelligence, Surveillance and Reconnaissance (C4ISR) Initiative

The countries of Southeast Asia, the Eastern Indian Ocean and the Southwest Pacific currently possess varying capabilities to detect, observe and understand sea and air movements in their maritime surrounds. This weakness has serious economic, environmental and security consequences for these countries because they are often unable to detect incidents of maritime pollution, accidents, illegal fishing, smuggling, armed robberies at sea, terrorist movements and interference with the seabed within their exclusive economic zones and their broader maritime approaches. They also generally have a limited appreciation of military and para-military activities that external states are undertaking in their regions. This essay recommends that Australia launch a sustained initiative in partnership with the countries of maritime Southeast Asia, the Eastern Indian Ocean and the Southwest Pacific to significantly improve this situation during the coming decade.

Some regional countries and the US have already taken modest steps to improve maritime domain awareness.[39] The intent of this

---

39 See, for example, discussion of the operations of the Information Fusion Centre in Singapore, the ASEAN information-sharing portal, Indonesia's National Maritime Security Information Centre and India's Information Management and Analysis Centre in, Ristian Atriandi Supriyanto *Waves of Opportunity: Enhancing Australia-Indonesia Maritime Security Cooperation* (Strategic Insights 79, November 2014); Dr Ely Ratner, 'China and the Evolving Security Dynamics in East Asia: Security Dynamics in East Asia: Security Dynamics in Southeast Asia and Oceania and Implications for the United States,' (Testimony Before the US-China Economic and Security Review Commission, 13 March 2014) p. 7; http//origin.www.usoc.gov/sites/default/files/transcripts/Hearing%20Transcript_March%2013.2014_0.pdf Accessed on 18 June 2015 and Vijay Sakhuja *Indian Ocean: Exploring Maritime Domain Awareness* (Institute of Peace and Conflict Studies, New Delhi, Article 4825, 2, February 2015) @ http://www.ipcs.org/print_article-details.php?recNo=4853 (Accessed on 14 February 2015).

proposal is to partner with all regional countries to build on existing arrangements, extend them significantly and markedly improve capacities to network surveillance systems across the region. This should permit the generation of a common operational picture of the regional maritime domain, markedly improve regional transparency and facilitate more efficient maritime operations by all partners.

3. Establish the Indo-Pacific Exercise and Range Complex

One of the serious problems confronting most of Australia's allies and close security partners in the Indo-Pacific is the difficulties they experience in accessing a comprehensive network of military exercise and range facilities. This is a growing problem for the U.S, especially as it proceeds to position 60 per cent of its naval and air forces in this theatre. Relocating these naval, air, army and marine forces to the Pacific is one thing but maintaining them in this theatre in a high state of readiness for long periods of time is another challenge altogether.

Japan also has serious problems accessing suitable facilities for many types of complex training. Most Japanese maritime and air exercises are confined to limited offshore zones and many major ground force manoeuvres are conducted on the northern island of Hokkaido.

India and most of Australia's security partners in Southeast Asia have similar problems, which are likely to be exacerbated as urban encroachment places new restrictions on national exercise facilities and realistic training with many modern sensor and weapons systems requires access to much larger areas.

Australia has a competitive advantage in exercise and range

facilities which it could use to strengthen its security partnerships with allies and friends. Australia already possesses exercise and range areas that are large, relatively uncluttered and feature diverse air, sea and land environments. Several of these offer training within instrumented networks, featuring wide-area unit tracking, recording and play-back facilities. Some also provide exercise options in remote and secure locations. All of them are supported by first-world maintenance and repair facilities.

Amongst the more notable training and exercise facilities are:

- Shoalwater Bay coastal training complex in central Queensland.
- Delamere instrumented air combat range in the Northern Territory.
- Bradshaw exercise area on the northwest coast of Western Australia.
- Woomera weapons range and training area in central Australia.
- Naval range facilities on both the east and west coasts of the continent.

This essay is not suggesting unrestricted foreign access to Australia's exercise and range facilities. The ADF will always wish to retain priority access. Moreover, environmental factors constrain the use of some ground manoeuvre and other exercise areas in order to ensure soil, watercourses and vegetation have time to recover from damage. However, offering Australia's close allies and friends periodic, and possibly regular, access to certain exercise and range facilities would be a powerful means of reinforcing the strength and special nature of these partnerships.

Consequently, this essay recommends that the Australian Government establish the Indo-Pacific Exercise and Range Complex (IPERC). This would be a network of current exercise and range facilities on and adjacent to Australia, backed by electronic simulation and other computerised training systems. Were international demand to require it, new exercise areas and facilities might be added to the complex over time. The IPERC would be accessible to visiting forces of close allies and security partners by prior arrangement on agreed terms and conditions.

There may be another valuable use for some range and exercise areas for the US and other close allies. The US is currently developing a number of new-technology military systems and advanced operating concepts as part of its new Offset Strategy. Many of them are being developed for primary employment in the Indo-Pacific region. There would be substantial benefits in testing and trialling their performance within the region for which they are designed. The IPERC would offer these advantages to the US within highly secure environments.

Establishing the Indo-Pacific Exercise and Range Complex in Australia would greatly assist the US achieve its rebalancing and Offset Strategy goals. It would make extended American force deployments to Australia and its surrounding region much easier, more effective and less expensive.

The creation of this exercise and range complex would also assist Australia's other security partners in the Indo-Pacific build their skills, strengthen their operational readiness and bolster their strategic confidence.

4. Establish an Australia-US Strategic Planning Group

Earlier parts of this essay discussed the strategic significance of the rise of China and other Indo-Pacific powers and the fact that the centre of major power competition, and potentially of conflict, is now closer to Australia's north. As a result of these and related developments, both US and Australian defence planners are needing to rethink assumptions about future military operations in this theatre. Many aspects of tactics, operational concepts and strategy are under review. The Americans, in particular, appreciate they need significantly altered approaches for their new Offset Strategy in order to counter the anti-access, area denial capabilities being deployed by some countries.

In these changing strategic circumstances, this essay argues it is in Australia's interests to work more closely with the Americans to develop strategy and campaign options that best meet both countries' needs. This would deliver stronger leverage in Washington and across the region as well as the prospect of a stronger deterrence capacity and security for Australia.

Consequently, there would be benefit in forming a small, high quality, Australia-US Strategic Planning Group. Primary tasks for this combined staff could include designing, analysing and testing alternative campaign strategies and operational concepts, developing contingency plans in close cooperation with the joint operational planning staffs of each country and assessing the potential for joint development of priority new defence capabilities.

5. Refine Australian and Allied Campaign Strategies

While Australia has a strong and proud history of conducting effective military operations and winning many tactical victories, the country does not have a deep tradition of developing, discussing and debating advanced military strategy. There have been exceptional individual contributors to strategic thinking but they are few in number. Australia's defence and national security communities are not strategy-rich.

If Australia's limited skills for strategy and campaign development have generally been inadequate in the past, they are even more under-powered in the new strategic circumstances. With the centre of any future superpower conflict now closer, Australia has an even stronger interest than in the past in the game-plan for deterring future conflicts, countering forceful coercion and, if required, for fighting and winning. However, Australia is not likely to exert a strong influence on future allied strategy in the Indo-Pacific unless several initiatives are taken.

First, there is a need to infuse Australian defence planning with a much deeper appreciation of the demands of preferred theatre and campaign strategies.

Second, theatre strategy and campaign planning need to be high priorities in Australia's staff colleges. Particular attention should be accorded to lessons learned from recent campaigns. Leading international strategic thinkers should be engaged on these courses to discuss and debate the insightful work they have been doing on alternative campaign strategies for future crises in the Indo-Pacific.

Third, there is need to integrate Australia's (and the close allies') defence strategies into the selection of ADF capabilities, postures and actions, so that the evolving force offers the greatest potential to deter, effectively counter forceful coercion and, if necessary, defeat a major power opponent. A core aim of these strategies should be to force an opposing decision-making elite to change its mind and come to terms that are acceptable to Australia and its security partners.

Fourth, Australia needs to more effectively engage key US personnel in deep discussions on the advantages and disadvantages of different types of theatre strategy for the Indo-Pacific.

6. Establish Indo-Pacific Intelligence Hub

Many advantages would flow to Australia if it became the centre of intelligence excellence for the close allies in the Western Pacific and the Eastern Indian Ocean.

The aim of this initiative would be to exploit Australia's strong track record for generating quality intelligence products, its geo-strategic location, its high quality workforce, its technological sophistication and its political stability to become the undisputed leader in Indo-Pacific intelligence collection and assessment.

Developing Australia as the allied intelligence hub for the Indo-Pacific should lead to the country becoming the best-informed nation in the theatre. It would greatly enhance Australia's capability to conduct independent and allied military operations across the region. This initiative would also mean that on most mornings the President of the US and the leaders of other close allies would read Australian-sourced material in their daily intelligence briefs. Above all, it would reinforce in allied capitals Australia's status as a very special ally.

7. Establish Indo-Pacific Hub for Space and Allied C4 Operations

Australia has the potential to further strengthen its strategic value to the US and other close allies by working to expand its support for allied space and communications, command, control and computer (C4) operations.

This proposal builds on a long-standing strategic logic. During the early stages of the Second World War, General Douglas MacArthur, the Supreme Allied Commander in the Pacific, established his headquarters first in Melbourne and later in Brisbane. Australia was seen to be an ideal location for the Pacific theatre command headquarters. Operations on and from Australia into the Southwest Pacific, Southeast Asia and adjacent maritime areas were an order of magnitude easier and quicker than those launched from continental US. Because of Australia's vast size and terrain diversity it was seen as a formidable bastion, it was politically reliable and possessed a well-trained English-speaking workforce. In addition, MacArthur realised Australia offered strong industrial capabilities and well-developed communications and transport facilities. It was an ideal command location while allied forces recovered from the disasters of Pearl Harbour and Singapore and restored their strategic and operational balance.

With the arrival of the space age in the 1950s and 60s Australia and the US agreed to build joint space support facilities at Pine Gap, near Alice Springs, and Nurrungar, near Woomera. Now, with the US considering a range of new space-based and C4 programs as part of its developing Offset Strategy, the Australian Government can offer access for a new generation of jointly operated facilities. This has the potential to significantly boost allied operational capabilities in the Indo-Pacific and strengthen allied command resilience.

8. Enhance Cyber and Special Operations Capabilities

Effective management of cyberspace will be a key factor in almost all future security operations in the Indo-Pacific. If Australia and its allies and friends are to deter, defend against and, if necessary, defeat future cyber criminals, terrorist groups and hostile states, they will need strong and resilient capabilities in this field. Hence, there should be two main cyber elements in Australia's strategy of partnership and leverage.

First, Australia must strengthen defensive and offensive cyber capabilities, partly by expanding cooperation with the US and other close allies.

Second, Australia should extend its efforts to develop cooperative cyber security programs with key regional partners, particularly in maritime Southeast Asia, largely to help strengthen their cyber defences and build national economic and security resilience.

9. Develop Combined Air, Naval and Ground Force Support Presence

The Pentagon is facing major dilemmas as it contemplates optimal operating and basing modes in the Western Pacific for the coming half century. There are several drivers for change.

First, there is a consensus in the US defence community that current American strategy in the Western Pacific is unsustainable. The challenge posed by the advanced anti-access, area denial capabilities being deployed by China requires the development and testing of new campaign strategies and tactics.

Second, the US plans to relocate most of its forces to the Asia-Pacific by 2020 and this may over-stretch its bases in the region.

Third, most American combat aircraft deployed to the Pacific have relatively short operating ranges. When deployed to the current poorly located, restricted capacity and inflexible basing structure in the Western Pacific, their operational capabilities are limited.

Fourth, the current American basing structure in the Western Pacific is too concentrated and does not facilitate an adequate degree of protected force dispersal, rendering the units at current facilities vulnerable to surprise attacks.

Fifth, some US bases in Japan, especially those on Okinawa, are politically contentious. Not all local communities are welcoming of a continued American military presence.

Sixth, opportunities for US forces to undertake some types of training and exercises in the theatre are limited by the nature and location of current facilities.

In these circumstances, Australia offers numerous basing and force dispersal options for air, naval, ground, marine and other defence units. Australia also has modern defence facilities, strong industrial support capacities and a well-developed civil infrastructure. Importantly, American service personnel rate Australia as one of the most desirable overseas locations to visit and so postings 'down-under' rarely impact adversely on personnel retention.[40]

American defence planners appreciate there are political sensitivities in Australia about conventional styles of US military basing. They also understand the forms, terms and conditions of any expanded US military access to Australia would have to be

---

[40] See, for example, the remarks by Captain Karl Thomas, the commanding officer of the USS *Carl Vinson* as he approached the Australian coast on 26 April 2015. Andrew Burrell 'Fresh from Battle, R&R now on the Radar' *The Australian* (27 April 2015) p. 4.

agreed in a consensual manner with the three major Australian political parties.

Given the Liberal, National and Labor Parties are all long-standing supporters of the ANZUS Alliance and of effective combined defence operations, the prospects of reaching effective and durable agreements are good. Nevertheless, there is a need to tread carefully, brief fully, discuss all options openly and ensure that not only ministers, shadow ministers and senior officials understand key issues but so do other parliamentarians, media organisations and most members of the general public.

Australia already hosts extended deployments of US Marine contingents to Darwin that are scheduled to expand to a 2,500-strong Marine Air-Ground Task Force by 2020. In addition, there are periodic visits by US Air Force and Navy units for exercises, rest and recreation and other purposes – with few problems encountered. What might now be sensible to contemplate are extended deployments to expanded Australian facilities of US Air Force and Navy units as well as pre-positioning additional US defence equipment to support future exercise and operational activities.

One prospective approach would be to operate selected US air and naval units out of Australian facilities for extended periods, with the aircraft and ship crews and support staff periodically rotated back and forth to their families in the US. An alternative, and probably preferred approach in the long term, would be for some Australian and American units to have a permanent joint operating presence at new facilities in carefully selected locations that can house, service and maintain defence systems and personnel from both countries. There should be significant economic benefits to Australia, especially for the supply of construction, maintenance, repair, logistic supply, transport and tourism services. Key issues are likely to include appropriate arrangements for the sharing of costs and consultation prior to the conduct of combat and other sensitive operations on or from Australian territory.

The long-term stationing of US air, naval and ground combat forces in Australia would greatly ease the basing pressure being experienced by American forces in the Western Pacific and provide a much firmer and more resilient allied operating presence in the theatre. In effect, long-term forward stationing of American combat units in the country would underline Australia's role as a secure southern anchor and a strategic hinge between the Pacific and Indian Oceans.

10. Phased Development and Deployment of Next-Generation Ballistic Missile Defences (BMD)

A notable feature of several defence modernisation programs across the Indo-Pacific region is the development and deployment of medium and long range ballistic and cruise missile systems. It is no longer just the long-established nuclear powers that have fielded these offensive missile systems. Notable medium and long range missile forces are now operated in the Indo-Pacific region by Russia, China, North Korea, India and Pakistan. Other countries are expected to follow suit in the coming two decades.

Australian defence planners cannot ignore the prospect that these missile systems will be used in future conflicts in the region and that in some future wars Australian territory will be targeted. This challenge needs to be addressed in a realistic manner in the interests of all Australians and also in the interests of allies and friends who may operate defence assets from or around Australia in coming decades.

Against limited missile attacks the current generation of BMD systems have been shown to be reasonably effective.[41] However, all of these systems are very expensive and the scope for providing effective BMD cover for all potential targets in Australia using existing technologies is limited.

The medium-term outlook for BMD systems is, however, more encouraging. Important advances in space-based systems, lower cost high-power radars, electro-magnetic rail guns, new technology high-power lasers and other systems appear likely to offer more cost-effective BMD options in the coming two decades. Because of Australia's technological depth in some of these newer technologies there may be opportunities to participate in the American-led design, development and testing of next-generation BMD systems. In the medium to longer term, it may be also feasible for Australia to deploy some of these more cost-effective BMD systems.

11. Become the Close Allies' Indo-Pacific Arsenal

The potential for Australia to serve as an allied arsenal in the event of major crises and conflicts dates from the Second World War. During the early phases of that conflict several notable Americans visited Australia and were impressed by the speed and effectiveness with which a wide range of military equipments were put into production, including several types of combat aircraft, tanks and warships. One of the most influential of these American visitors was Mr Carroll Binder, a senior journalist with the *Chicago*

---

41 Australia's three new Air Warfare Destroyers will have a basic ballistic missile defence capability for limited areas if their radars and fire control systems are given a software upgrade, if they are equipped with SM-3 interceptor missiles and if they are located appropriately and are alert at the time of a regional ballistic missile launch.

Daily News. Binder, on his return to the U.S, wrote several articles and delivered a succession of speeches about the importance of supporting Australia as the arsenal of the Pacific theatre.[42]

This line of thinking appears to have been noted by several senior officials serving the Roosevelt Administration. One of these was Admiral Ernest King, who, in early 1942, was appointed Commander in Chief, US Fleet (the equivalent of the current Chief of Naval Operations). Admiral King had the ear of the President and he argued strongly and very persuasively that holding Australia and New Zealand must be an early priority of allied strategy.

The logic then was that Australia and New Zealand were robust defensive bastions that offered secure bases, advanced maintenance, repair, and resupply facilities, strong manufacturing capabilities and that they were sound locations from which allied forces could concentrate and launch counter-offensive operations to the north.

With global strategic attention now returning to the Indo-Pacific, the possibility of Australia again serving as an allied arsenal is receiving new attention. Australia's manufacturing sector now produces a much narrower range of products than in the 1940s but it is still capable of designing and building surprisingly advanced systems and products when required. There is also a possibility that the innovative use of super computing, advanced robotics, 3D printing and other new technologies may give the country's manufacturing sector a second wind. Were that to occur, Australia would not only reap substantial economic benefits but it would also generate a powerful extra layer of strategic value to the close allies.

---

42 See, for example, Carroll Binder *Australia: Arsenal of the Pacific* (A speech delivered to the Chicago Council on Foreign Relations, Palmer House, Chicago, 20 February 1941). Text supplied on request by the Newberry Library, Chicago, 12 August 2014.

12. Strengthen Australia's High Leverage Combat Capabilities

For most of Australia's history the threat environment has been low and close allies have carried much of the load. In these circumstances the penalties for loose priorities and limited discipline in defence investments have been modest.

A clear conclusion of this essay is that those relaxed days are over. The changes in Australia's security environment mean defence planners need to sharpen defence investment priorities to focus on those that contribute substantially to Australia's deterrence and defensive leverage in those contingencies that are critical for national survival.

What then should be the key characteristics of the country's future capability priorities?

- they should be strategy-driven and selected for their capability to play key roles in applying leverage against opposing decision-making elites;
- they must be capable, survivable and sustainable in high intensity conflict;
- when appropriate, they must mesh seamlessly with US forces and contribute significantly to allied combat capabilities in the Indo-Pacific theatre;
- the future ADF must be backed by well-protected basing, logistic and reserve force capabilities that can be mobilised quickly; and
- they should be able to bolster regional partner deterrence and defensive capabilities at short notice.

Conclusions

This essay argues Australia's grand strategy must move into a new era. The challenge of providing effective security for Australia has been demanding in the past but it is now truly daunting.

Australia suffers from a mismatch between its geographic scale and its defence resources. The Australian continent is a similar size to the continental US. Australia also has several offshore territories that are as far from the mainland as Hawaii is from North America. Australia's population, economy and tax base are, however, comparable to Texas. This means that Australia needs to secure itself with a defence budget that is less than one-fortieth that which is available to the Pentagon. This funds a permanent defence force that numbers just over half a Melbourne Cricket Ground crowd. Hence, a central challenge for Australian defence planners is how to strengthen deterrence and defensive capabilities in the more demanding strategic environment now developing when its independent resources are so limited.

At the same time, Australia's geo-strategic location is now close to the centre-stage of superpower rivalry and a likely region for any future major war. Australia is no longer a strategic backwater and its strategy and security planning need to be restructured appropriately.

Australia is now of greatly increased geo-strategic importance to both the US and also to a number of rapidly rising powers. While some Australians might prefer to distance themselves from heightened major power competition, such tensions are taking an increasing and unavoidable interest in Australia.

Several important consequences flow for Australian defence planning.

First, Australia may be confronted in the future by conflict initiated by major powers located in Australia's region. Moreover, the nature and form of such coercion and conflict would probably be markedly different from the more limited contingencies that have driven Australian defence planning for the last forty years.

Second, there is no sound basis for assuming that Australia will receive an extended period of clear warning prior to a major conflict in the Indo-Pacific. Australian defence planning needs to assume that unless capabilities can be operational within a month they may have little relevance for the initial phases of such a conflict.

Third, were a major conflict to erupt between the major powers in the Indo-Pacific, its duration may not be short. Indeed, it could extend for many months or even years.

Largely as a result of the above factors, Australia's close ally, the US, now has a much stronger interest in operating on and from Australia in close partnership with the ADF.

Many regional countries share Australia's concerns about the changing strategic situation. If the government takes up the resulting opportunities to develop closer security partnerships across the Indo-Pacific, Australia may have more opportunities to shape a favourable strategic environment than at any other time in its history.

In order to respond effectively to the markedly different strategic circumstances now developing this essay argues six key steps need to be taken.

First, the Australian Government must explain to the community the changing nature of the country's security challenges and the need to take new defensive measures.

Second, the government needs to re-state the country's core security objectives and define a new grand strategy that is tailored for the more challenging times ahead. This essay argues that partnership and leverage would be an effective grand strategy for the new era.

Third, the government needs to re-state its commitment to spend a minimum of 2 per cent of GDP on defence so as to strengthen Australia's independent capabilities to defend the country's most vital security interests.

Fourth, in order to greatly strengthen Australia's deterrence, and also the credibility of the US extended deterrence commitment, Australia should offer to host a wide range of American combat and combat support units in Australia on a permanent basis. This would greatly ease American basing pressures, reduce the prospect of conflict escalation and take the Australian-American alliance to a new level. Australia should strive to become the indispensable American ally in the Indo-Pacific.

Fifth, Australia needs to refocus and re-energise its programs to strengthen strategic partnerships with a range of priority regional countries, especially Japan, China, South Korea, India, Indonesia Malaysia, the Philippines, Papua New Guinea and the island states of the Southwest Pacific.

Sixth, Australia needs to strengthen its domestic resilience to prepare for potential energy, food, biological, chemical and cyber security challenges in the years ahead.

In short, it is time for Australians to become much better informed about the markedly different strategic landscape that is developing. Australians need to look beyond their domestic preoccupations and debate the best ways of strengthening the country's security for the more demanding times ahead.

It's time for Australians to lift their game.

Acknowledgements

This essay would not have been possible without the encouragement, advice and assistance of many senior leaders in the Australian and US national security communities. Two high-level closed workshops were conducted in Canberra to discuss the primary themes in the essay and review draft documentation. While different views were expressed at various stages, a clear consensus emerged on the key judgements. The contributions of these senior national security leaders were extremely valuable and greatly appreciated.

Special thanks are also due to Nick Cater, the Executive Director of the Menzies Research Centre, who kindly arranged for the essay to be released in the Menzies Research Centre's R.G. Menzies Essay series and to Stephen Matchett, who provided substantial editorial assistance.